THE HIGH
BLOOD-PRESSURE
COOKBOOK

Reduce the Risk of Heart Disease and Stroke With a 28-Day Meal Plan: Delicious Recipes to Enhance Heart Health and Effectively Lower Blood Pressure

Optima Health Institute

TABLE OF CONTENTS

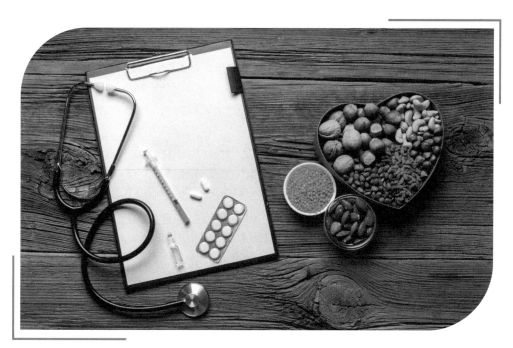

INTRODUCTION

According to global statistics, approximately 1.28 billion people aged between 30 and 70 have high blood pressure (World Health Organization (WHO), 2023). About two-thirds of these people are from low- and middle-income countries. Although high blood pressure is regarded as one of the major causes of premature death globally, only 42% of the people who live with this condition have been properly diagnosed and treated (WHO, 2023). This means that more than half of the affected people may not be aware they have it or are not receiving relevant interventions. This further increases the risk of death, but what does the phrase "high blood pressure" really mean?

For you to survive, your blood should circulate to all parts of your body to supply them with oxygen. Your blood also collects the waste products of metabolism so that your body cells continue functioning efficiently. Blood movement is aided by some level of pressure inside the blood vessels. When the pressure in your blood vessels exceeds normal levels, the condition is referred to as high blood pressure, or hypertension. You might be wondering how the blood pressure is measured. Whenever hypertension is tested, you will see two numbers, one over the other. The number on top measures the systolic blood pressure.

This is the pressure with which blood flows through the arteries, which are the vessels that transport blood from the heart. The systolic pressure is associated with your heartbeat. The lower number represents the diastolic pressure, which measures the force of blood flow between one heartbeat and the next. The unit of measurement for blood pressure is mmHg.

If you're above 18 years old, your normal blood pressure should be 120/80 mmHg. This means that the systolic and diastolic pressure should be 120 and 80 mmHg, respectively. As you can see, the systolic pressure should be higher than the diastolic pressure. This is because the diastolic pressure represents the resting state of your heart. Once your systolic pressure exceeds 120 mmHg, it's too high. The same applies when the diastolic pressure rises beyond 80 mmHg. When your blood pressure rises beyond the normal, you may experience one or more of the following symptoms:

- Weakness
- Breathing difficulties
- Numbness
- Talking difficulties
- Bleeding nose
- Extreme anxiety

- Abdominal pain
- Chest pain
- Vision challenges

Whether you are preparing for life after bariatric surgery or living day one of that life, this bariatric diet cookbook is here to equip you with everything you need for success. With a balance of long-term keys to success and tips for managing your immediate needs, gone are the days of wondering whether you are doing what's best for your health. With this book, you will be able to seamlessly adapt your eating habits and food choice to support your new lifestyle and continuous health goals. So, what are you waiting for? Let's dive into your new diet, starting right now!

Once you experience any of these symptoms, we recommend that you call 911 or seek medical attention. If not addressed, high blood pressure opens doors to more health complications. For example:

- Fluid may accumulate in your lungs, thereby interfering with breathing efficiency.
- You may experience seizures, especially when you have eclampsia or are pregnant.
- The pressure may cause your aorta to tear. The aorta is the largest artery, responsible for taking oxygenated blood from the heart to other parts of your body.
- Your brain may bleed or swell.
- You may experience a stroke.

Types of High Blood Pressure

High blood pressure can be classified based on its causes. This gives rise to two groups:
- **Primary hypertension:** This is also known as essential hypertension. In this case, there is no specific cause for elevated blood pressure. However, the blood pressure tends to progressively increase over time until it becomes a condition that requires

attention. Therefore, primary hypertension is often associated with hereditary factors. The genes for this condition may follow the bloodline.
- **Secondary hypertension:** In this case, high blood pressure is a result of another condition. For instance, diabetes may cause some blood vessels to stiffen, a factor that can cause high blood pressure.

Diet and Blood Pressure

Have you ever heard of the old adage that says, "You are what you eat"? The components of your diet significantly contribute to the state of your health. More specifically, the compounds in the food that you eat may help to manage high blood pressure. Some foods may even worsen the situation. For instance, research has shown that a diet that involves foods rich in fats, added sugar, and refined carbohydrates might increase your chances of developing high blood pressure (Ozemek et al., 2018). In contrast, whole grains and other plant-based foods are effective in preventing and managing hypertension. Therefore, a healthy diet is one of the most effective interventions for high blood pressure.

Take Charge!

This book takes you through the journey of using your diet to deal with hypertension. It begins by providing you with the information that helps you understand what high blood pressure entails. It then explains how you can use your diet as a tool for combating high blood pressure. The 28-day meal plan in this book will give you practical footing for creating your own recipes and "anti-hypertension" meal plans. This book also highlights the importance of mindful eating and intuitive eating in fighting high blood pressure. In essence, it's not just about the food but the eating process as well. Now, take the bull by the horns and use this double-edged strategy to develop an edge over high blood pressure. Take charge and keep this condition at bay!

CHAPTER 1

Understanding Blood Pressure and Your Body

The pressure at which your blood flow changes throughout the day to meet your body's needs. For instance, when you work out, the pressure might increase as the heart tries to supply your muscles and body cells with enough oxygen to cope with the increased activity. However, your blood pressure shouldn't exceed certain levels if you are to maintain a state of good health. In this chapter, we will help you understand how blood pressure works so that you are in a better position to control it.

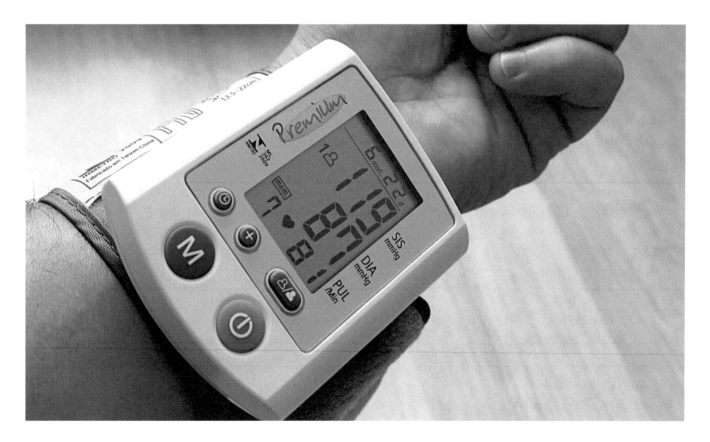

How Blood Pressure Works

High blood pressure is best determined when you are resting. The table below shows the ranges that you can use to establish whether your blood pressure is within normal levels.

Interpretation	Systolic Pressure (mmHg)	Diastolic Pressure (mmHg)
Optimal	Below 120	Below 80
Normal	120 to 129	80 to 84
High-normal	130 to 139	85 to 89
High	Above 140	Above 90

The table shows that your blood pressure is normal when the systolic pressure is within the range of 120 to 129 mm/Hg and the diastolic pressure is between 80 and 84 mmHg. You don't have to worry if your blood pressure is within these levels. You may begin to get concerned if systolic and diastolic pressure rise to around 139 and 89 mmHg, respectively. However, these pressure levels are not as dangerous as in cases where the systolic and diastolic pressures are above 140 and 90 mmHg, respectively. Under these circumstances, there is no doubt that you are hypertensive.

Factors Influencing Blood Pressure

As mentioned earlier, blood pressure can fluctuate, which is due to various factors, some of which we will explore in this section.

- **Stress:** When you're stressed, your blood pressure is more likely to rise. Chronic stress may cause you to be a hypertension patient in the long run.
- **Medication:** Changes in your blood pressure may be due to the medications that you are taking. Some medications cause your blood pressure to spike while others lower it.
- **Diet:** What you eat and drink has a lot to do with your blood pressure levels. For instance, foods that are rich in tyramine are more likely to raise your blood pressure beyond normal ranges (Burns and Kidron, 2020). Caffeinated drinks also temporarily cause your blood pressure to spike. Other foods, including those that are rich in potassium, are effective in lowering your blood pressure.
- **Activity:** Any form of activity, be it exercise, sex, laughing, or talking, can cause blood pressure spikes.
- **Issues associated with the adrenal system:** The adrenal system is the one responsible for producing different hormones. When there are problems with this system, fluctuations in blood pressure can result. For example, adrenal insufficiency may cause low hormones to be produced, further leading to reduced blood pressure.

While these are the general factors that determine your blood pressure at any given time, there are parameters that put you at an increased risk of hypertension. These include the following:

- **Lifestyle issues:** If your lifestyle triggers stress, anxiety, and depression, this increases your risk of having to deal with high blood pressure. Night-shift work may cause hypertension associated with sleeplessness. Heavy alcohol consumption also increases the risk of hypertension.

- **Underlying conditions:** There are health conditions that are associated with high blood pressure. These include diabetes, kidney disease, cardiovascular disease, and obstructive sleep apnea. The nervous system, thyroid, and kidney issues can also raise the probability of having high blood pressure.
- **Stages of life:** When you are pregnant, high blood pressure may be an issue.

High Blood Pressure, Heart Disease, and Stroke: The Connection

When you're hypertensive, the risk of heart disease and stroke is also relatively higher. This is because hypertension can cause a lot of damage to your heart system.

Heart Disease

Heart disease exists in three forms, all of which are linked to high blood pressure in one way or another. These are as follows:

- **Coronary artery disease:** In this case, high blood pressure damages the arteries that transport oxygenated blood to your heart. As a result of the damage, inadequate blood flows to the heart muscle. This comes with various symptoms, such as chest pain and irregular heartbeats. In worst-case scenarios, coronary artery disease can lead to a heart attack.
- **Heart attack:** In the event that you experience high blood pressure for extended periods, your blood vessels may endure damage. Tiny tears can develop on the walls of the blood vessels. In an effort to repair these tears, your body will release special cells that will stick to the affected areas. Bad cholesterol may also build up on the same spots, resulting in the formation of plaque that blocks the flow of blood. Blockage of blood vessels may deprive certain regions of the heart of oxygen and nutrients that are necessary for survival. This is what is called a heart attack.
- **Heart failure:** High blood pressure causes your heart to put more effort into pumping blood. As a result, the walls of the chamber that pumps blood thicken, which negatively affects its capacity to pump enough blood to take care of your body's needs. This condition is referred to as ventricular hypertrophy. The condition may worsen to the extent that the heart will fail to supply the body with enough blood. This is a state of heart failure.

Stroke

When high blood pressure damages the blood vessels that are connected to the brain, the probability of stroke increases. In this case, the blood vessels may become too narrow to supply enough blood to the brain. They may even become blocked, which deprives some parts of the brain of the oxygen and nutrients necessary for survival. Waste products of metabolism also accumulate in a similar manner because they cannot be removed due to the blockage. Once this happens, a stroke results.

The Role of Nutrients

Did you know that nutrition has a role to play in regulating your blood pressure? This means that different nutritional components have different effects on your blood pressure. They may raise or lower the pressure. In this section, we will explore some of the key nutrients involved in controlling blood pressure. These include the following:

- **Sodium:** Sodium encourages water retention, thereby increasing the volume of your blood. This results in increased blood pressure.
- **Potassium:** One of the roles of potassium in your body is to help your blood vessels to relax. This has the effect of reducing blood pressure. Potassium is also involved in the conduction of electric signals between your nervous system and your heart. This keeps your heart beat regular. An irregular heart beat may also interfere with the blood pressure levels. There are foods that naturally contain high amounts of potassium, including apricots, lima beans, and sweet potatoes. Green leafy vegetables and fish such as salmon are rich in potassium.
- **Calcium:** Calcium helps your blood vessels to relax and contract when necessary, and this affects blood pressure levels.
- **Magnesium:** Magnesium also controls your blood pressure by causing your blood vessels to relax. Dark-green leafy vegetables are among the excellent sources of magnesium.

Omega-3 fatty acids affect blood pressure in an indirect way. These are healthy fats that your body needs. Omega-3 fatty acids increase the levels of good cholesterol (high-density lipoproteins) while reducing that of bad cholesterol (low-density lipoproteins). Bad cholesterol increases the chances of fatty blockages in blood vessels, which could otherwise promote high blood pressure.

Nutrients that regulate your blood sugar levels also control your blood pressure in the long run. This is because excess glucose is often converted to and stored as fat. This can lead to obesity, which may increase the risk of having to deal with high blood pressure.

This chapter explored the basics of what blood pressure entails and how it affects your cardiovascular system. We also highlighted the key nutrients that raise or lower your blood pressure. This shows why your diet is an important factor in regulating your blood pressure. In the next chapter, we will look into the fundamentals of intuitive eating.

CHAPTER 2

Intuitive Eating Fundamentals

Intuitive eating is an approach to food consumption during which you pay attention to how your body defines hunger and satiation. You see, it is more than an eating event. In other words, intuitive eating recognizes the connection between your body's senses, the food, and the eating process. You need to train yourself to eat intuitively. However, don't expect to master everything at once. Keep practicing and you will get a hang of it. This chapter will help you understand what intuitive eating entails.

The Art of Listening to Your Body's Hunger and Fullness Cues

Quite often, we confuse hunger with cravings. You don't have to be hungry to crave a certain food. Cravings can be triggered by the smell or appearance of food, so you may end up eating for the sake of it, even when you're not really hungry. Cravings are an example of external cues that encourage eating.

It's crucial to connect to your body's signs of hunger and fullness. There are many ways to tune in to these internal hunger and satiation cues. Let's explore some of the strategies that may work for you.

Pay More Attention to Eating

Allowing distractions when you eat can interfere with your ability to connect with your body's cues. Remember, you tune in to these signs using your senses. Watching your screens, reading, and/or talking when you're eating shifts some of your senses away from focusing on the eating process. Therefore, it's vital that you learn to concentrate on your food

and the whole act of eating. This will help you understand how the food makes you feel while you continue eating. As you continue doing this at every meal, you will gradually get acquainted with how your body reacts when you're hungry or full.

Connect With Physical Hunger Cues

Hunger signals are quite personal, though there are some signs that are relatively common to different people. You might experience any of the following:

- Feeling faint or light-headed
- Stomachache or headache
- Growling or rumbling stomach
- Losing concentration on tasks at hand

It's important to determine how your body tells you that it's hungry. There are some factors that may interfere with your hunger cues. For example, when you're overwhelmed with tasks at work or home, you might not pay attention to your body's hunger signals. Another factor is related to what you eat. For instance, diet sodas and calorie-free foods tend to fill your stomach up without providing your body with the energy it requires. This can confuse your body into assuming that it's full, yet it's not gaining much. We recommend that you eat nutritional foods that will make it easier for you to realize when you're hungry.

Understand Other Hunger Types

If you don't experience the cues that are often associated with your hunger, you're more likely to experience nonphysical hunger. You could be having emotional or mental hunger. Emotional hunger is when you eat based on your feelings. For instance, you may eat as a way of dealing with anger, anxiety, stress, or depression. Mental hunger may be a response to the senses of sight and smell with regard to certain foods. You might buy a doughnut just because you saw one and it appealed to your senses. You should know that both mental and emotional hunger cannot be quenched by eating because they are not related to physical cues. Train yourself not to yield to emotional and mental hunger; otherwise, you will fill your tummy with unhealthy foods that cause high blood pressure, among other problems.

Get in Touch With Satiation Cues

How does your body tell you that you are full? Here are some nuggets that will assist you in realizing your satiation cues:

- ☼ Take note of how your stomach feels as you continue to eat.
- ☼ Slow down when eating so that you acknowledge the sensations associated with satiation.
- ☼ Determine your energy levels as you eat. Ideally, you should feel energetic. Once you start feeling tired, it might be a sign that you're too full already.
- ☼ Divide your food into smaller portions. Only go for the next portion when you're certain that you still feel hungry.

Use a Numerical Scale

A numerical scale can be helpful in determining the level of your hunger or satiation. In this case, you rate your hunger or satiation on a scale that ranges from 1 to 10. The table below shows an example of a scale that you can use.

Points	Description	Diagnosis
1	Feeling dizzy and weak	Extremely hungry
2	Lower energy levels and growling stomach	Very hungry
3	Slight growls in the stomach	Pretty hungry
4	Lower energy levels	A little hungry
5	Neutral feelings	Satisfied
6	Feeling pleasantly full	A little full
7	Feeling uncomfortable inside your stomach	Very full
8	Feeling very stuffed	Too full
9	Painful stomach	Uncomfortably full
10	Feeling sick as a result of overeating	Extremely full

Awareness of the Effects of Different Foods

Every food has its distinct effects on your body and overall health. This is why it's crucial to know which foods to eat. Contextually, some foods support your goal of keeping your blood pressure in check while others are unhealthy for your cardiovascular system.

Foods to Eat

Here are some of the foods that you should consider including in your diet if you want to lower your high blood pressure:

- **Berries:** Berries, including strawberries and blueberries, are rich in compounds called anthocyanins. Research has shown that these compounds can reduce high blood pressure (Vendrame and Klimis-Zacas, 2019).
- **Leafy green vegetables:** The nitrates in these vegetables make them great for alleviating high blood pressure. Research has confirmed the positive effects of leafy green vegetables on your heart system (Bondonno et al., 2021). Therefore, include spinach, kale, and cabbage in your diet.
- **Lentils:** Scientific studies have confirmed that fiber and protein in lentils are beneficial when it comes to controlling your blood pressure (Hartley et al., 2022).
- **Beets:** Beets contain dietary nitrate, which is converted to nitric oxide once inside your body. Nitric oxide makes your blood vessels relax, thereby reducing high blood pressure. This has been confirmed by research (Benjamim et al., 2022).
- **Tomatoes:** Tomatoes have lycopene, which is an antioxidant. Lycopene has positive effects on your cardiovascular system.
- **Garlic:** Research has revealed that garlic can reduce bad cholesterol levels, arterial stiffness, and blood pressure (Ried, 2019).

- **Citrus fruits:** These fruits harbor an antioxidant called hesperidin, which is good for the health of your heart system.
- **Bananas:** Bananas are rich in potassium, one of the minerals that help your blood vessels to relax. You can also find potassium in lentils, squash, and potatoes.
- **Oats:** Oats contain beta-glucan, a type of fiber that is beneficial for your blood pressure. One study reported the important role of beta-glucans in enhancing cardiovascular health (Wouk et al., 2021).
- **Fermented foods:** Fermented foods such as tofu, miso, and tempeh have been reported to significantly lower the risk of high blood pressure (Yoo and Park, 2020).
- **Nuts:** You can never go wrong by including nuts in your diet—they are effective in lowering hypertension.
- **Oily fish:** Fish such as tuna and salmon have omega-3 fatty acids, the effects of which contribute to lowering high blood pressure.

Foods to Avoid

Avoid foods that cause spikes in blood pressure. Here are some of such foods:

- **Salt:** Salt contains sodium, which causes your blood pressure to rise.
- **Alcohol:** When consumed regularly, alcohol elevates your blood pressure.
- **Caffeine:** Caffeine supports hypertension. It may even cause complications in hypertension patients when taken regularly. in hypertension patients when taken regularly.
- **Processed foods:** Processed foods are rich in harmful fats that increase the risk of atherosclerosis, which is the accumulation of bad cholesterol in blood vessels.

The Art of Slow and Mindful Eating

Eating slowly is connected to mindful eating. Why? Because when you eat slowly, you give yourself the chance to pay more attention to the food. It's easier to take note of the taste, smell, appearance, and texture of your food when you eat at a slower pace. Did you also know that slow and mindful eating contributes to alleviating high blood pressure? Here is how this happens:

○ **It enhances digestion.** When you eat slowly, you get enough time to chew your food. This marks the beginning of the proper digestion of food. No matter how beneficial your food could be to blood pressure, it only serves its purpose when it has been properly digested. Digestion makes the relevant nutrients available for absorption into your body.

○ **It promotes nutrient absorption.** Slow eating provides enough time for digestion and the ultimate absorption of nutrients. The minerals and other nutrients that can lower your blood pressure become available for use in the body.

○ **It lowers the risk of metabolic syndrome.** Research has shown that eating at a fast pace elevates the risk of metabolic syndrome (Zhu et al., 2015). This refers to a cluster of conditions that include high blood sugar levels and hypertension.

○ **It reduces weight gain.** Eating fast is associated with possible overeating—hence, weight gain. It's easy to eat more than you should when you're eating quickly. Therefore, slowing down may contribute to weight loss, which is a sign of reduced accumulation of fats. This reduces the risk of atherosclerosis and possible high blood pressure.

Alvin Toffler once said, "The illiterate of the twenty-first century will not be those who cannot read and write, but those who cannot learn, unlearn, and relearn" (Amdur, 2022). This chapter encouraged you to relearn your hunger and fullness signals. We also highlighted the foods that you should eat and avoid if you want to manage blood pressure levels in your body. This chapter dove into how you can incorporate intermittent fasting and mindful eating into your diet.

CHAPTER 3

Incorporating Mindful Eating and Intermittent Fasting

We discussed a little about mindful eating in the previous chapter. However, this chapter introduces intermittent fasting, which is another important technique that might give you an edge over high blood pressure. Together, intermittent fasting and mindfulness form a holistic approach to cardiovascular health. In essence, this chapter will explore how you can address blood pressure from a holistic point of view.

The Role of Mindful Eating in Managing Blood Pressure

Mindfulness refers to the art of tuning in to the present moment, which can increase your awareness of your surroundings and what is happening in and around you. Mindfulness helps you to make healthy choices with regard to the food that you eat. Mindful eating helps you to focus on eating lean proteins, whole grains, fruits, and vegetables, all of which are supportive of a healthy heart system.

Mindfulness helps you adhere to a heart-healthy diet. The results from one study showed that the high blood pressure patients who took part in a mindfulness program could better stick to a healthy diet than those who didn't (Loucks et al., 2023). Apparently, the positive effects of mindfulness were achieved in two ways:

- **Improved self-awareness:** Mindfulness assisted the participants in connecting with their inner selves. It helped them understand and value themselves better. The participants became more acquainted with their hunger and satiety signals. This puts them in a better position to make good and informed decisions regarding their diet. As the participants became more self-aware, they understood their emotions better. This helped them to avoid embracing negative relationships between food and emotions. Emotional and mental eating can be avoided when such a state is achieved.
- **Better eating habits:** As a result of increased self-awareness, the participants embraced healthier eating habits. These include eating slowly, avoiding distractions during meal time, and eating in response to true hunger, not to mention consuming the right foods.

In essence, mindful eating is supportive of healthy levels of blood pressure. It increases the chances that you will eat foods that maintain normal blood pressure levels.

Safe Approaches to Intermittent Fasting

Intermittent fasting involves eating at designated periods of time and refraining from food the rest of the time. Therefore, intermittent fasting is described in terms of eating and fasting windows, both of which are quite self-explanatory. However, it's important to note that for a heart-healthy diet, only foods that support your cardiovascular system should be considered during your meals. Intermittent fasting gives your body more time to burn calories. This is why this method is often used as a weight-loss strategy. Some also use it for regulating blood sugar. By the way, excess blood glucose is converted to fat, which is then stored in your body. The fasting window ensures that there is no extra glucose to store as fat. Not only that, as the fasting goes on, your body will turn to the fatty reserves for its energy supply. As the accumulated fat gest used up, weight reduces, blood sugar is controlled, and ultimately, blood pressure is also regulated.

Here are some of the intermittent approaches that you can try:

- **The 5:2 method:** In this approach, you eat your heart-healthy foods for five days of the week. You can select two days during which you can fast.
- **Time-restricted fasting:** In this form of intermittent fasting, you decide your eating and fasting times every day of the week. For example, you can choose to eat from 9 a.m. to 5 p.m. and fast the rest of the time. In this case, this means you will have to eat your dinner earlier so that you honor the fasting period. This intermittent fasting approach is good because you won't have to technically miss meals. Apparently, the better part of the fasting period is covered during your sleeping time. This may enhance the efficiency of metabolism. Please note that experts recommend that women avoid fasting for more than 14 hours each day.
- **Overnight fasting:** This is also referred to as 12:12 fasting and it implies that you fast for 12 hours and resume eating for the same length of time. For instance, you can start eating at 7 a.m. and have your dinner just before 7 p.m. You don't eat anything the rest of the night. Apparently, overnight fasting is regarded as the simplest among all types of intermittent fasting.

Other forms of intermittent fasting, including whole-day fasting and eat-stop-eat, require you to refrain from eating for 24 hours. This may be too long if you have blood pressure issues. Sometimes, your blood pressure may drop too low. If you are on medication for high blood pressure, you might need to eat before taking the pills. This makes 24-hour fasting methods not ideal for your condition. Fasting for too long may also interfere with the electrolyte balance in your body. This may cause your heart to have irregular rhythms, further contributing to significant and possibly dangerous fluctuations in blood pressure. We recommend that you book an appointment with your doctor to discuss the fasting approaches that work best for you.

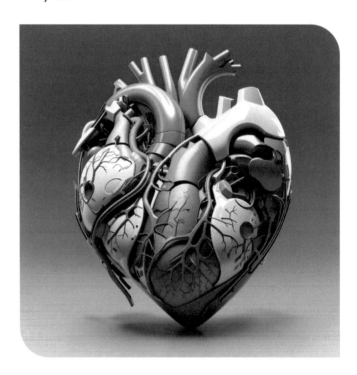

The Role of Intermittent Fasting in Cardiovascular Health

You might be surprised at what intermittent fasting can do for your cardiovascular system. This practice helps to do these three things:

- **Aid weight loss:** Fasting gives your body enough time to use the glucose in the blood. Once it's depleted, your body cells will depend on glycogen stores in the liver for energy. After that, your body turns to the fatty reserves. This means that fasting can reduce the accumulation of fatty reserves. Weight gain is mainly attributed to the build-up of fats in your body, which ensures that stored fat is used up. Intermittent fasting aids weight loss and helps to reduce obesity. Research has established a connection between obesity and hypertension (Shariq and McKenzie, 2020). By reducing obesity and weight gain, intermittent fasting reduces the risk of high blood pressure.

☼ **Reduce cholesterol levels:** Intermittent fasting reduces your eating time. This literally means reducing the time for binging, as well as emotional and mental eating. This reduces glucose spikes in the blood, thereby also alleviating the conversion of sugar to fats. If you combine intermittent fasting with mindful eating, you are more likely to consume healthy fats during your eating window. This also assists in lowering the bad cholesterol levels in your body. Lower cholesterol levels reduce the risk of atherosclerosis. This protects you from high blood pressure.

☼ **Enhance insulin sensitivity:** Insulin is the hormone that enhances the uptake of glucose from the blood by body cells for use in metabolism. Sometimes, body cells may become insensitive to insulin, as is the case with type 2 diabetes patients. Experimental results have revealed that intermittent fasting improves the cells' sensitivity to insulin (Yuan et al., 2022). When body cells are insensitive to insulin, the blood is flooded with glucose, which will ultimately be stored in the form of fats. By improving insulin sensitivity, intermittent fasting prevents fat from accumulating in your body.

This chapter discussed intermittent fasting as well as mindful eating. We explored the various types of intermittent fasting that you can consider. However, fasting for 24 hours is not a good idea if you have blood pressure issues. Experts also suggest that women restrict their fasting windows to no more than 14 hours. Combined with mindful eating, intermittent fasting is an effective tool for regulating your blood pressure. In the next chapter, we will provide you with highlights of the meals that you will prepare during your 28-day meal plan.

CHAPTER 4
The 28-Day Meal Plan

This chapter is a preview of the 28-day meal plan for controlling your blood pressure. You will find the different recipes that you will eat for each meal for the next 28 days. The actual recipe descriptions for all the meals are available in Chapter 5.

Weekly Overviews

This section provides an overview of the meals you will prepare and eat for the next 28 days.

Week 1

Here are the meals for the first week:

	Breakfast	Lunch	Dinner	Snacks
Monday	Bagel Avocado Toast	White Bean Soup	Chickpea and Quinoa Grain Bowl	Cheddar-Apple Cracker Bites
Tuesday	Pineapple-Grapefruit Detox Smoothie	Seitan BBQ Sandwiches	Italian Zucchini–Topped Baked Potato	Smoked Salmon Toast
Wednesday	Banana Pancakes	Tangy Chicken Salad With Grapes	Tomato, Cucumber, and White Bean Salad With Basil Vinaigrette	Creamy Strawberry Smoothie
Thursday	Baby Kale, Smoked Trout, and Avocado Salad	Strawberry Spinach Salad With Avocado and Walnuts	Slow-Cooker Chicken and White Bean Stew	Cinnamon-Sugar Microwave Popcorn
Friday	Peanut Butter and Chia Berry Jam Muffin	Pork and Green Chile Stew	Veggie and Hummus Sandwich	Garlic Hummus
Saturday	Herbal Chamomile Health Tonic	Bean Salad With Lemon-Cumin Dressing	Broccoli Mac and Cheese With Rotisserie Chicken	Bread With Peanut Butter
Sunday	Southwestern Waffle	Crunchy Chicken and Mango Salad	Mixed Greens With Sliced Apple and Lentils	Hard-Boiled Egg With Sauce

Week 2

Here are the meals for the second week:

	Breakfast	Lunch	Dinner	Snacks
Monday	Herbed Ricotta and Cannellini Bean Toast	Chicken, Brussels Sprouts, and Mushroom Salad	BBQ Baked Potatoes With Pork and Broccoli	Cherry Tomato and Egg Cracker
Tuesday	Spinach, Banana, and Peanut Butter Smoothie	Greek Salad With Edamame	Saucy Ginger-Tomato Chicken	Savory Date and Pistachio Bites
Wednesday	Creamy Blueberry-Pecan Oatmeal	Charred Shrimp, Pesto, and Quinoa Bowls	Black Bean Tacos and Roasted Vegetables	Raspberry Yogurt Cereal Bowl
Thursday	Portobello Mushrooms Florentine	Rainbow Grain Bowl With Cashew Sauce	Smoked Salmon–Stuffed Baked Potatoes	Avocado Hummus
Friday	Lemon Flaxseed Parfaits	Miso-Maple Salmon	Tex-Mex Pasta Salad	Tuna Salad Crackers
Saturday	Spinach and Egg Scramble With Raspberries	Southwest Chopped Salad With Tomatillo Dressing	Smoked Turkey, Kale, and Rice Bake	Walnuts and Banana
Sunday	Breakfast Sweet Potatoes	Shrimp Paella	Southwestern Salad With Black Beans	Pumpkin Pie Smoothie

Week 3

Here are the meals for the third week:

	Breakfast	Lunch	Dinner	Snacks
Monday	Pear and Pecan Butter Toast	Baked Fish Tacos With Avocado	Marinara Meat Sauce–Topped Baked Potato	Almond-Stuffed Dates
Tuesday	Raspberry-Mango Smoothie	Loaded Black Bean Nacho Soup	Salmon Couscous Salad	Carrot Cake Energy Bites
Wednesday	Egg Tartine	Red Beans and Rice With Chicken	Lemon-Garlic Vegetable Soup	Mint, Lemon, and White Bean Dip
Thursday	Yogurt With Honey and Blueberries	Lemony Linguine With Spring Vegetables	Creamy Pesto Chicken Salad With Greens	Rice Cakes with Peanut Butter
Friday	Old-Fashioned Oatmeal	Chicken and Beet Salad	Pan-Seared Steak With Crispy Herbs and Escarole	Chocolate-Banana Protein Smoothie
Saturday	Ginger-Orange Tea	Grilled Blackened Shrimp Tacos	Lemon Shrimp and Orzo Salad	Cinnamon-Sugar Roasted Chickpeas
Sunday	Berry Granola Pancakes	Teriyaki Chicken Skillet Casserole With Broccoli	No-Cook Black Bean Salad	Cottage Cheese Snack Jar

Week 4

Here are the meals for the fourth week:

	Breakfast	Lunch	Dinner	Snacks
Monday	Peach and Pistachio Toast	Cabbage, Tofu, and Edamame Salad	Mason Jar Power Salad With Chickpeas and Tuna	Apple With Cinnamon Almond Butter
Tuesday	Banana-Berry Cauliflower Smoothie	Chickpea Pasta With Mushrooms and Kale	Black Bean and Slaw Bagel	Blueberry-Lemon Energy Balls
Wednesday	Muesli With Raspberries	Classic Sesame Noodles With Chicken	Green Goddess Salad With Chickpeas	Homemade Trail Mix
Thursday	Spiced Blueberry Quinoa	Mushroom and Tofu Stir-Fry	Hearty Tomato Soup With Beans and Greens	Hard-Boiled Egg and Almonds
Friday	Whole-Wheat Pancakes	Colorful Mixed Salad	Cream of Turkey and Wild Rice Soup	Almond Chia Blueberry Pudding
Saturday	Southwest Tortilla Scramble	Walnut-Rosemary Crusted Salmon	Eat-the-Rainbow Vegetable Soup	Peanut Butter–Banana Cinnamon Toast
Sunday	Carrot Cake Oatmeal	Chopped Power Salad With Chicken	Chicken Chili Verde	Yogurt and Fruit Smoothie

Now that you have all the recipes at your disposal, go ahead and get the information on how to prepare them in the next chapter.

CHAPTER 5

Recipes for Heart Health

Let's get practical! Think of this chapter as a reservoir for the various recipes that will make up your 28-day meal plan for addressing blood pressure. You will get breakfast, lunch, dinner, and snack recipes with ingredients that can lower your blood pressure. The effects of the various ingredients are attributed to the compounds they contain. Find out more as you go through the recipes!

BREAKFAST
RECIPES

Find the breakfast recipes in this section.

Bagel Avocado Toast

 Serving Size: 1   Total Time: 5 minutes

We can't talk of heart-healthy ingredients without mentioning avocados, which are a rich source of omega-3 fatty acids. Eating avocados reduces your body's bad cholesterol (LDL) levels while increasing those of good cholesterol (HDL). This puts your cardiovascular system in a better state of health. One study reported that participants who ate a diet rich in avocados had significantly lower chances of having to deal with heart disease (Wang et al., 2019).

Nutritional Facts

172 calories	18 g carbohydrates
5 g proteins	10 g fats

Ingredients:

- 2 teaspoons bagel seasoning
- 1/4 medium avocado, mashed
- A pinch of flaky sea salt
- 1 slice whole-grain bread, toasted

Instructions:

1. Spread the mashed avocados on the toast slice.
2. Sprinkle the seasoning and salt on top.
3. Enjoy!

Pineapple-Grapefruit Detox Smoothie

 Serving Size: 2   Total Time: 10 minutes

Did you know that potassium is involved in regulating your blood pressure? Well, pineapples are rich in this mineral, along with fiber, which also reduces bad cholesterol levels in your body. The grapefruit alleviates inflammation and also helps your body maintain normal levels of blood pressure.

Nutritional Facts

102 calories   25 g carbohydrates
2 g proteins   0 g fats

Ingredients:

- ✿ 1 small grapefruit, peeled and segmented
- ✿ 1 cup plain coconut water
- ✿ 1 cup pineapple, frozen and diced
- ✿ 1 cup ice
- ✿ 1 cup baby spinach
- ✿ 1/2 teaspoon fresh ginger, grated

Instructions:

1. Add all the ingredients to a blender.
2. Process until the ingredients are smooth and homogeneously mixed.
3. Enjoy!

Spinach and Egg Scramble With Raspberries

 Serving Size: 1   Total Time: 10 minutes

Here is an interesting fun fact—Did you know that spinach has more fiber, vitamin A, and protein? The compounds that are found in spinach make this vegetable handy in enhancing the health of your heart. Adding eggs and raspberries to the recipes is an incredible plus!

Nutritional Facts

296 calories   21 g carbohydrates
18 g proteins   16 g fats

Ingredients:

- 1 slice whole-grain bread, toasted
- 1 teaspoon canola oil
- A pinch of kosher salt
- 2 large eggs, lightly beaten
- A pinch of ground pepper
- 1 1/2 cups baby spinach
- 1/2 cup fresh raspberries

Instructions:

1. Place a skillet over medium-high heat and add oil to it.
2. Add spinach to the skillet and cook for approximately 2 minutes. Stir regularly.
3. Transfer the cooked spinach to a plate and clean the skillet.
4. Add eggs to the skillet and cook over medium heat for about 2 minutes. Stir occasionally as you cook the egg.
5. Add the spinach, pepper, and salt. Mix well.
6. Serve along with raspberries and toast.
7. Enjoy!

Creamy Blueberry-Pecan Oatmeal

 Serving Size: 2   Total Time: 10 minutes

Reports from research have revealed the various benefits that oatmeal has on your cardiovascular system (Llanaj et al., 2022). For example, oatmeal contains manganese, whose roles in blood clotting and cholesterol metabolism cannot be ignored. This is partly attributed to the beta-glucan found in oats. Oatmeal is also rich in fiber, a characteristic that is important in reducing the unnecessary consumption of extra calories. Such regulation of food consumption supports the health of your heart.

Nutritional Facts

291 calories   49 g carbohydrates
9 g proteins   8 g fats

Ingredients:

- 1/2 cup old-fashioned rolled oats
- A pinch of salt
- 2 teaspoons pure maple syrup
- 1 tablespoon pecans, toasted and chopped
- 1/2 cup blueberries, fresh
- 2 tablespoons nonfat plain Greek yogurt
- 1 cup water

Instructions:

1. Add the salt and water to a saucepan and bring to a boil.
2. Reduce the heat and add oats. Cook for around 5 minutes while stirring occasionally. Almost all the liquid should be absorbed by then.
3. Remove the saucepan from the heat and cover it for about 3 minutes.
4. Top with pecans, blueberries, syrup, and yogurt.
5. Enjoy.

Peach and Pistachio Toast

 Serving Size: 1   Total Time: 5 minutes

Take charge of your blood pressure and heart rate by including peaches in your diet. Peaches have good amounts of potassium, a mineral that is supportive of your heart health. Pistachios have similar effects, which are mainly attributed to the antioxidants they contain.

Nutritional Facts

262 calories   41 g carbohydrates
10 g proteins   9 g fats

Ingredients:

- ☼ 1 teaspoon honey, divided
- ☼ 1 tablespoon part-skim ricotta cheese
- ☼ 1 slice 100% whole-wheat bread, toasted
- ☼ 1/8 teaspoon cinnamon
- ☼ 1 tablespoon chopped pistachios
- ☼ 1/2 medium peach, sliced

Instructions:

1. Add cinnamon, ricotta, and 1/2 teaspoon of honey to a small bowl. Mix well.
2. Spread the mixture from Step 1 on top of the toast.
3. Add pistachios and peach on top of the ricotta mixture on the toast.
4. Drizzle the remaining honey and enjoy!

Carrot Cake Oatmeal

 Serving Size: 8   Total Time: 6 hours 10 minutes

You probably know that carrots are good for eye health. However, did you also know that they support the health of your heart? This effect is partly due to the potassium content of carrots. Carrots also contain lycopene, a compound that helps to prevent heart disease.

Nutritional Facts

197 calories   46 g carbohydrates
4 g proteins   2 g fats

Ingredients:

- 2 cups carrots, shredded
- 1 teaspoon pumpkin pie spice
- 20-ounce crushed pineapple, undrained
- 1 cup steel-cut oats
- 2 teaspoons ground cinnamon
- 1 cup raisins
- 4 1/2 cups water

Instructions:

1. Coat the slow cooker with cooking spray.
2. Add all the ingredients to the slow cooker.
3. Cook on low for about 8 hours. The oats should be tender by then.
4. Serve and enjoy!

Peanut Butter and Chia Berry–Jam Muffin

 Serving Size: 1   Total Time: 10 minutes

This is a fiber-rich breakfast! The chia seeds, whole-wheat muffin, and berries all offer fiber in this recipe, which effectively reduces the amount of bad cholesterol in your body. They make you feel satiated for longer periods, thereby reducing your glucose intake. This means there will be less glucose available for conversion to fats. This protects you from obesity and lowers the chances of heart disease.

Nutritional Facts

262 calories   41 g carbohydrates
10 g proteins   9 g fats

Ingredients:

- ☼ 2 teaspoons natural peanut butter
- ☼ 2 teaspoons chia seeds
- ☼ 1/2 cup unsweetened mixed berries, frozen
- ☼ 1 whole-wheat muffin, toasted

Instructions:

1. Add the berries to a microwave-safe bowl. Microwave the berries for about 30 seconds. Stir and microwave for 30 more seconds before adding the chia seeds. Stir again.
2. Carefully spread the peanut butter on the muffin.
3. Add peanut butter on top of the peanut butter.
4. Enjoy!

Breakfast Sweet Potatoes

 Serving Size: 4   Total Time: 55 minutes

In this meal plan, anything that reduces bad cholesterol levels is a plus, which is why you should consider including sweet potatoes to this recipe. This breakfast also includes apples, which have been scientifically proven to reduce the chances of high blood pressure and heart disease (Sandoval-Ramírez et al., 2020).

Nutritional Facts

321 calories	70 g carbohydrates
7 g proteins	3 g fats

Ingredients:

- 1/4 cup toasted unsweetened coconut flakes
- 4 medium sweet potatoes
- 2 tablespoons maple syrup
- 1 medium apple, chopped
- 1/2 cup fat-free coconut Greek yogurt

Instructions:

1. Preheat your oven to 400 °F.
2. Line your baking sheet with foil. Arrange the sweet potatoes on the baking sheet. Bake for about an hour until the potatoes appear soft.
3. Cut the sweet potatoes as if you're making an "X" on each of them.
4. Fluff the pulp using a fork.
5. Top using the rest of the ingredients.
6. Enjoy!

Egg Tartine

 Serving Size: 4 Total Time: 10 minutes

An egg a day is good for your heart; this has been confirmed by extensive research (Harvard Health Publishing, 2019). It's also wise to take advantage of the potassium in tomatoes. Potassium helps to relax your blood vessels, thereby relieving high blood pressure. This mineral also removes some sodium from your blood. Sodium causes high blood pressure while increasing the risk of heart disease and stroke. Prepare this recipe and keep your heart system healthy!

Nutritional Facts

184 calories   14 g carbohydrates
10 g proteins   10 g fats

Ingredients:

- 2 tablespoons mixed herbs
- 1 1/2 teaspoons extra-virgin olive oil
- 4 large eggs, fried
- 1 medium tomato, sliced
- 4 slices whole-wheat bread, lightly toasted
- 1 garlic clove, halved
- 4 teaspoons capers, rinsed

Instructions:

1. Brush the olive oil onto the toast before rubbing garlic over it.
2. Add tomatoes and eggs over the toast.
3. Sprinkle the herbs and capers.
4. Enjoy!

Whole-Wheat Pancakes

 Serving Size: 20 pancakes   Total Time: 25 minutes

In one study, the participants who included whole wheat in their diet had significantly reduced blood pressure compared to those who didn't (Corliss, 2021). Whole wheat is also great for regulating blood sugar levels. Incorporate this heart-healthy ingredient into your diet by making whole-wheat pancakes!

Nutritional Facts

157 calories   24 g carbohydrates
9 g proteins   4 g fats

Ingredients:

- 2 cups whole-wheat flour
- 3 cups buttermilk
- 1/2 teaspoon salt
- 1 teaspoon baking soda
- 1/2 cup toasted wheat germ
- 2 large eggs
- 1 tablespoon canola oil

Instructions:

1. Add flour, baking soda, wheat gem, and salt into a bowl. Mix well.
2. Add buttermilk, oil, and eggs in a separate bowl. Whisk to combine.
3. Add the wet-ingredient mixture into the bowl with dry.
4. Coat a griddle with cooking spray and heat it.
5. Measure quarter-cupfuls of the batter and put them in the hot griddle.
6. Cook until bubbles appear on top of the pancakes.
7. Turn the pancakes and cook again until the bottom appears golden brown.
8. Enjoy!

Herbed Ricotta and Cannellini Bean Toast

 Serving Size: 2   Total Time: 10 minutes

For good heart health, you need foods that are rich in folate. This is vitamin B, which your body uses to make red blood cells. Remember, red blood cells are the ones that carry oxygen to different parts of your body. Therefore, a diet rich in folate enhances the efficiency of oxygen transportation around your body. Now, the better part is that cannellini beans are an excellent source of folate, making this recipe exactly what you've been looking for!

Nutritional Facts

320 calories   42 g carbohydrates
15 g proteins   9 g fats

Ingredients:

- 2 tablespoons red bell peppers, chopped and roasted
- 2 slices seeded sourdough bread, toasted
- 2 tablespoons chopped mixed fresh herbs
- 1 cup rinsed, no-salt-added canned cannellini beans, heated
- 1/2 cup part-skim ricotta cheese

Instructions:

1. Add the herbs and ricotta to a small bowl. Mix well.
2. Divide the mixture into 2 parts. Spread each part of the mixture on one toast slice.
3. Add 1/2 cup of the cannellini beans to each toast slice. Also, share the peppers between the slices and sprinkle them over the beans.
4. Enjoy!

Ginger-Orange Tea

 Serving Size: 4 pancakes   Total Time: 15 minutes

If you prefer a much lighter breakfast, a cup of healthy tea will do you good. Research has shown that ginger has potent cardioprotective effects (Fakhri et al., 2021). Apart from preventing hypertension, ginger can prevent platelets from causing blood clots in the bloodstream, which protects you from a possible stroke or heart attack. Ginger also helps regulate blood cholesterol levels. This, along with the antioxidant properties of the orange juice, makes the ginger-orange tea a good treat for your heart.

Nutritional Facts

11 calories   3 g carbohydrates
0 g proteins   0 g fats

Ingredients:

- ✿ 4 green tea bags
- ✿ 1/4 cup orange juice
- ✿ 4 cups water
- ✿ 1 1-inch piece fresh ginger, peeled and thinly sliced

Instructions:

1. Boil the water in a saucepan before reducing the heat.
2. Add the ginger slices and tea bags to the saucepan. Cover with a lid and let the ingredients steep for about 4 minutes.
3. Discard tea bags from the tea mixture.
4. Add the orange juice and stir. At this point, you can remove the ginger slices. However, you can keep them if you prefer a more intense flavor.
5. Pour the tea into 4 cups and enjoy!

Old-Fashioned Oatmeal

 Servings: 1   Total Time: 15 minutes

Oatmeal can do a lot for your heart. For instance, the beta-glucan in oats lowers the total cholesterol in your body. It also improves good cholesterol levels while reducing bad cholesterol levels. The oatmeal also helps to control blood sugar levels, and this reduces the accumulation of unwanted fat, some of which could build up around your heart muscle and blood vessels. This could lead to a condition called atherosclerosis, which further increases the risk of high blood pressure, heart disease, and stroke. Use this recipe to make your oatmeal and enjoy the heart-related benefits!

Nutritional Facts

150 calories   27 g carbohydrates
5 g proteins   3 g fats

Ingredients:

- 1/2 cup rolled oats
- A pinch of cinnamon
- 1 cup water
- A pinch of salt
- 2 teaspoons honey
- 2 tablespoons low-fat milk (for serving)

Instructions:

1. Add salt and water to a saucepan and bring to a boil.
2. Reduce the heat to medium, and then add oats. Cook for 5 minutes while stirring.
3. Remove the saucepan from the heat and let it stand for around 3 minutes while covered.
4. Top with cinnamon, honey, and milk.
5. Enjoy!

Muesli With Raspberries

 Servings: 1   Total Time: 5 minutes

Did you know that beta-glucan can lower the cholesterol levels in your body by 2% (El Khoury et al., 2012)? More interestingly, muesli is a rich source of beta-glucan. Therefore, by eating this meal, you are setting your heart up for better health!

Nutritional Facts

288 calories   52 g carbohydrates
13 g proteins   7 g fats

Ingredients:

- 1 cup raspberries
- 1/3 cup muesli
- 3/4 cup low-fat milk

Instructions:

1. Add raspberries to muesli.
2. Serve along with milk.
3. Enjoy!

Spinach, Banana, and Peanut Butter Smoothie

 Servings: 2   Total Time: 5 minutes

Prepare this smoothie and regulate your blood pressure in a more natural way! Spinach is great for regulating blood pressure. Bananas contain antioxidants that may protect you from cancers that are related to the cardiovascular system. Peanut butter contains a type of fat called oleic acid. These fats control cholesterol and blood sugar levels.

Nutritional Facts

324 calories   45 g carbohydrates
16 g proteins   11 g fats

Ingredients:

- ☼ 1 cup plain kefir
- ☼ 1 frozen banana
- ☼ 1 tablespoon honey
- ☼ 1 cup spinach
- ☼ 1 tablespoon peanut butter

Instructions:

1. Mix all the ingredients in a blender and process.
2. Once you get a smooth product, serve and enjoy!

Berry Granola Pancakes

 Servings: 18   Total Time: 20 minutes

The antioxidant activity exhibited by berries is beneficial to your heart system. Just like oatmeal, granola also contains beta-glucan, which protects your blood vessels by preventing the accumulation of bad cholesterol. These pancakes are not only healthy, but they also taste great!

Nutritional Facts

275 calories   9 g carbohydrates
10 g proteins   23 g fats

Ingredients:

- 2 cups whole-wheat flour
- 1/2 teaspoon salt
- 2 cups fat-free milk
- 4 teaspoons baking powder
- 1 cup fresh or frozen blueberries
- 2 large eggs
- 1/2 teaspoon vanilla extract
- 3 tablespoons sugar
- 1 tablespoon canola oil
- 1 cup granola with fruit and nuts
- 1/2 cup fresh blackberries
- 1/3 cup unsweetened applesauce

Instructions:

1. Add the flour, baking powder, salt, and sugar. Whisk the ingredients together.
2. Add the oil, applesauce, eggs, vanilla, and milk into a separate bowl. Whisk again.
3. Add the wet ingredients to the dry. Slightly mix, just until the dry ingredients appear a little moistened.
4. Fold in berries and granola.
5. Use cooking spray to coat a griddle and place it on medium heat.
6. Measure 1/4 cup of the batter and put it on the griddle. Repeat until the griddle is full, but be sure to leave enough space between the batter mounds.
7. Cook until the bottom appears golden brown. Turn and cook the other side.
8. Repeat until all the batter is finished.
9. Serve and enjoy!

Baby Kale, Smoked Trout, and Avocado Salad

 Servings: 1   Total Time: 15 minutes

Kale is one of the ingredients that reduce the levels of unhealthy LDL cholesterol in your body. It is rich in minerals such as folate, calcium, and potassium, all of which support good heart health. Trout is an oily fish rich in omega-3 fatty acids. You know what that means, right?—reduced bad cholesterol levels.

Nutritional Facts

275 calories   9 g carbohydrates
10 g proteins   23 g fats

Ingredients:

- 3 cups baby kale
- 1 teaspoon garlic, minced
- 1/4 firm ripe avocado, sliced or diced
- A pinch of salt
- A pinch of pepper
- 2 teaspoons red wine vinegar
- 1/4 cup flaked smoked trout
- 1 tablespoon extra-virgin olive oil
- 1 tablespoon red onion, finely chopped

Instructions:

1. Add garlic and salt to a small bowl and mash them together. Transfer this paste to a medium bowl.
2. Add pepper, oil, and vinegar to the garlic paste.
3. Add kale and toss the ingredients together.
4. Top with avocado, trout, and red onions.
5. Enjoy!

Raspberry Mango Smoothie

 Servings: 1   Total Time: 5 minutes

Raspberries and mangoes contain potassium, which has been scientifically proven to be effective in lowering high blood pressure (Ellison and Terker, 2015). These berries also harbor omega-3 fatty acids, which promote better heart health. Mangoes are also rich in magnesium, which helps your heart maintain a regular pulse.

Nutritional Facts

188 calories   32 g carbohydrates
2 g proteins   7 g fats

Ingredients:

- 3/4 cup mango, frozen
- 1/2 cup water
- 1 tablespoon lemon juice
- 1 tablespoon agave (optional)
- 1/4 cup raspberries, frozen
- 1/4 medium avocado

Instructions:

1. Put all the ingredients in a blender.
2. Blend until consistently smooth.
3. Serve and enjoy!

Southwestern Waffle

 Servings: 1   Total Time: 10 minutes

The various ingredients in salsa can effectively reduce inflammation and LDL cholesterol levels. Such ingredients include tomatoes, peppers, and onions. Here is another interesting fact—eggs are associated with a reduced probability of having to deal with some types of stroke (Tang et al., 2020).

Nutritional Facts

207 calories	17 g carbohydrates
9 g proteins	12 g fats

Ingredients:

- 1 frozen whole-grain waffle
- 1 tablespoon fresh salsa, refrigerated
- 1/4 medium avocado, halved, peeled, and chopped
- 1 egg, cooked sunny-side up

Instructions:

1. Follow the package instructions to toast the waffle.
2. Add the egg on top of the waffle.
3. Top with the avocado and salsa.
4. Enjoy!

Herbal Chamomile Health Tonic

 Servings: 4   Total Time: 20 minutes

Chamomile prevents high blood pressure. It also relaxes your blood vessels when you're stressed, thereby making you feel more calm. However, avoid this tea if you're on blood thinners—chamomile increases the risk of bleeding under such circumstances. Adding rosemary to this tea is a plus. This herb improves blood circulation, further regulating your blood pressure.

Nutritional Facts

6 calories   1 g carbohydrates
0 g proteins   0 g fats

Ingredients:

- 4 cups boiling water
- 2 sprigs rosemary, lightly bruised
- 2 teaspoons grated fresh ginger
- 6 bags chamomile tea
- 4 teaspoons honey
- 4 slices lemon

Instructions:

1. Add boiling water, rosemary, ginger, honey, tea bags, and lemon into a heatproof bowl. Slightly stir and let the ingredients steep for about 20 minutes.
2. Strain the liquid. Be sure to squeeze all the liquid from the tea bags.
3. Drink and enjoy!

Yogurt With Honey and Blueberries

 Servings: 2   Total Time: 15 minutes

If you're serious about changing your body's lipid profile for the better, include honey in your diet. Preparing this recipe is one way of doing that. Research has shown that honey can improve good cholesterol levels, thereby protecting you from possible heart-related issues (Alkhalifah et al., 2021). This effect is partly attributed to the fact that honey contains compounds such as flavonoids and phenolic acids, which have potent antioxidant properties.

Nutritional Facts

195 calories   25 g carbohydrates
2 g proteins   1 g fats

Ingredients:

- 1 cup nonfat plain Greek yogurt
- 1 teaspoon honey
- 1/3 cup blueberries

Instructions:

1. Put the yogurt in a serving bowl.
2. Put the blueberries on top before drizzling the honey.
3. Enjoy!

Southwest Tortilla Scramble

 Servings: 1   Total Time: 5 minutes

There is no doubt that fiber improves the availability of healthy cholesterol in your body, and this is important for improved heart health. Tortillas are among the fiber-rich foods that you should consider including in your diet. Along with the spinach, salsa, cheese, and eggs, this recipe is perfect for your breakfast as you journey toward better heart health.

Nutritional Facts

196 calories   16 g carbohydrates
17 g proteins   7 g fats

Ingredients:

- 1/4 cup chopped fresh spinach
- 2 large eggs
- 4 large egg whites
- 2 corn tortillas (6 inches), halved and cut into strips
- 1/4 teaspoon pepper
- 1/4 cup salsa
- 2 tablespoons shredded reduced-fat cheddar cheese

Instructions:

1. Add eggs, pepper, and egg whites into a bowl. Whisk the ingredients together.
2. Add the cheese, tortillas, and spinach. Stir the ingredients together.
3. Coat a skillet with cooking spray and place it over medium heat.
4. Pour the egg mixture into the skillet. Cook while stirring until the egg mixture appears thickened, with no visible liquid remaining.
5. Top with salsa, and enjoy!

Banana-Berry Cauliflower Smoothie

 Servings: 2   Total Time: 10 minutes

Berries are known as rich sources of antioxidants, which scavenge oxidative free radicals that may cause damage to your body's cells. Your cardiovascular system is also protected by these antioxidants. Cauliflower is a rich source of sulforaphane, which reduces LDL cholesterol levels. This helps to reduce the accumulation of fats in your blood vessels, which in turn lowers the risk of high blood pressure.

Nutritional Facts

149 calories   29 g carbohydrates
3 g proteins   3 g fats

Ingredients:

- 1 cup banana, sliced and frozen
- 1/2 cup mixed berries, frozen
- 2 teaspoons maple syrup
- 2 cups unsweetened plain almond milk
- 1 cup riced cauliflower, frozen

Instructions:

1. Add the banana, mixed berries, maple syrup, almond milk, and cauliflower into a blender.
2. Process for about 4 minutes.
3. Serve and enjoy!

Pear and Pecan Butter Toast

 Servings: 1   Total Time: 5 minutes

Pecan butter has monounsaturated fats, which are good for your heart. Besides, this butter makes you feel fuller for longer, which reduces your calorie intake and prevents the build-up of unhealthy fats. Pears are rich sources of anthocyanins, which have been scientifically proven to protect you from coronary artery disease. This is a condition that results from the accumulation of fats inside your arteries or on their walls.

Nutritional Facts

209 calories	25 g carbohydrates
5 g proteins	11 g fats

Ingredients:

- 1 tablespoon pecan butter
- 1/2 small pear, thinly sliced
- 1 slice whole-grain bread, toasted

Instructions:

1. Spread the pecan butter on the slice of toast.
2. Add the pear slices on top of the pecan butter.
3. Serve and enjoy!

Spiced Blueberry Quinoa

 Servings: 2   Total Time: 40 minutes

Quinoa is a fiber-rich food that is great for enhancing heart health. This ingredient also harbors various antioxidants. A study reported that antioxidants are associated with a reduced risk of coronary artery disease (Leopold, 2015). Therefore, eat this spiced blueberry quinoa and protect your heart!

Nutritional Facts

352 calories   59 g carbohydrates
9 g proteins   10 g fats

Ingredients:

- 1/4 teaspoon vanilla extract
- 2 cups unsweetened almond milk
- 2 tablespoons almonds, chopped and toasted
- 1/4 teaspoon salt
- 1/2 teaspoon ground cinnamon
- 1/2 cup quinoa, rinsed and well-drained
- 1 cup fresh blueberries
- 2 tablespoons honey

Instructions:

1. Add quinoa to a saucepan and place it on medium heat. Cook until the quinoa is slightly fried. This should take about 7 minutes.
2. Add cinnamon, almond milk, salt, and honey to the saucepan. Bring the ingredients to a boil.
3. Reduce the heat so that the ingredients simmer while stirring occasionally. In about 25 minutes, the quinoa should be tender.
4. Remove the saucepan from the heat before adding vanilla and blueberries.
5. Sprinkle almonds on the quinoa.
6. Serve and enjoy!

Portobello Mushrooms Florentine

 Servings: 2   Total Time: 25 minutes

Research has shown that portobello mushrooms are beneficial to your heart. These mushrooms can alleviate inflammation (Kim et al., 2019). They also enhance a healthier balance of good and bad cholesterol, thereby protecting your heart from heart disease. Portobello mushrooms have been reported to reduce the risk of developing atherosclerosis (Kim et al., 2019). Enjoy the portobello mushrooms florentine, along with its "hearty" benefits!

Nutritional Facts

170 calories   9 g carbohydrates
12 g proteins   10 g fats

Ingredients:

- 2 large portobello mushrooms without stems
- 1 small onion, chopped
- 1/8 teaspoon pepper
- 2 large eggs
- Cooking spray
- 1 cup fresh baby spinach
- 1/8 teaspoon salt
- 1/2 teaspoon olive oil
- 1/4 cup crumbled goat cheese
- 1/8 teaspoon garlic salt

Instructions:

1. Preheat your oven to 425 °F.
2. Use the cooking spray to spritz the mushrooms before arranging them on a baking pan with the stem side facing upward.
3. Sprinkle pepper and garlic salt over the mushrooms.
4. Bake the mushrooms for about 10 minutes until they become tender.
5. Add oil to a nonstick skillet over medium-high heat. Saute the onion until it becomes soft before adding the spinach. Cook further until the spinach wilts.
6. Add salt and eggs into a bowl and whisk. Add the mixture to the skillet and cook while stirring.
7. Once there is no more liquid egg, add the mushrooms.
8. Sprinkle the cheese and enjoy!

Banana Pancakes

 Servings: 2   Total Time: 15 minutes

The banana-egg combo is excellent for enhancing heart health. Come to think of it, just one medium-sized banana will give you an average of 360 mg of potassium. Apparently, this content is enough to meet 10% of your body's daily potassium requirements (Parmar, 2022). Potassium plays a crucial role in regulating blood pressure.

Nutritional Facts

124 calories   14 g carbohydrates
7 g proteins   5 g fats

Ingredients:

- 1 medium banana
- 2 large eggs

Instructions:

1. Add bananas and eggs to a blender. Puree these ingredients until they appear consistently smooth.
2. Lightly oil a skillet and place it over medium heat.
3. Add 4 mounds of the banana batter into the pan. Each mound should be made up of 2 tablespoons of the batter.
4. Cook the batter mounds for about 4 minutes. The edges should appear dry by then.
5. Flip the pancakes and cook for 2 more minutes.
6. Remove the cooked pancakes from the pan and make more using the remaining batter.
7. Serve and enjoy!

Lemon-Flaxseed Parfaits

 Servings: 4   Total Time: 15 minutes

This recipe is rich with ingredients that support your heart's health. For example, research showed that flaxseed contains alpha-linolenic acid, which can significantly reduce high blood pressure (Khalesi et al., 2015). Lemons have vitamin C, which has antioxidant attributes and reduces the risk of heart disease and stroke (Joshipura et al., 2001; Yokoyama et al., 2000).

Nutritional Facts

214 calories   33 g carbohydrates
13 g proteins   4 g fats

Ingredients:

- 1/4 cup agave honey
- 2 teaspoons grated lemon zest
- 1 cup fresh raspberries
- 1 teaspoon vanilla extract
- 2 cups reduced-fat plain Greek yogurt
- 2 tablespoons ground flaxseed
- 2 tablespoons lemon juice
- 1 cup fresh blueberries

Instructions:

1. Add the vanilla extract, lemon juice, Greek yogurt, lemon zest, honey, and flaxseed into a bowl. Mix well.
2. Divide the yogurt mixture into two parts. Share the first half among 4 custard cups.
3. Use half of the berries to top the yogurt mixture in each custard cup.
4. Add the remaining yogurt mixture and finish up with the remaining berries.
5. Enjoy!

LUNCH RECIPES

Find the lunch recipes in this section.

Pork and Green Chile Stew

 Servings: 6   Total Time: 4 hours 25 mins

Take advantage of the capsaicin in green chile. This compound effectively reduces the accumulation of cholesterol. Capsaicin also regulates blood pressure.

Nutritional Facts

180 calories   23 g carbohydrates
15 g proteins   4 g fats

Ingredients:

- 2 pounds boneless pork sirloin roast or shoulder roast, cut into 1/2-inch pieces
- 3 cups water
- 4 cups peeled and cubed potatoes
- 1 tablespoon vegetable oil
- 1/2 teaspoon ground cumin
- 1 15-ounce can hominy or whole-kernel corn, drained
- 1/2 cup chopped onion
- 1/4 teaspoon dried oregano, crushed
- 1 teaspoon garlic salt
- 2 4-ounce cans diced green chile peppers, undrained
- 1/2 teaspoon ancho chile powder
- 2 tablespoons quick-cooking tapioca
- 1 tablespoon fresh cilantro, chopped
- 1/2 teaspoon ground pepper

Instructions:

1. Add oil into a skillet and cook half of the meat until it appears brownish. Transfer to a plate and cook the rest of the meat along with onions. Drain off any fat.
2. Put all the meat and onions into a slow cooker.
3. Add potatoes, tapioca, garlic, green chile peppers, oregano, cumin, ancho chile powder, hominy, salt, and water into the slow cooker. Stir to mix and cover. Cook on High for 4 hours.
4. Garnish with cilantro and serve.
5. Enjoy!

Greek Salad With Edamame

 Servings: 4   Total Time: 20 minutes

Here is another recipe with edamame, which is rich in the blood pressure–lowering mineral—potassium.

Nutritional Facts

344 calories   20 g carbohydrates,
17 g proteins   23 g fats

Ingredients:

- 1/4 teaspoon salt
- 1/4 cup red-wine vinegar
- 8 cups chopped romaine
- 3 tablespoons extra-virgin olive oil
- 1 cup halved cherry or grape tomatoes
- 1/4 teaspoon ground pepper
- 1/2 cup crumbled feta cheese
- 16 ounces frozen shelled edamame
- 1/4 cup sliced Kalamata olives
- 1/2 European cucumber, sliced
- 1/4 cup slivered red onion
- 1/4 cup slivered fresh basil

Instructions:

1. Whisk pepper, oil, vinegar, and salt in a bowl.
2. Add the remaining ingredients. Toss to coat before serving.
3. Enjoy!

Charred Shrimp, Pesto, and Quinoa Bowls

 Servings: 4   Total Time: 25 minutes

The quinoa, shrimp, and pesto all contribute toward lowering cholesterol levels in your body. This ultimately helps to control blood pressure.

Nutritional Facts

429 calories   29 g carbohydrates,
31 g proteins   22 g fats

Ingredients:

- 1 pound peeled and deveined large shrimp (16-20 count), patted dry
- 1 tablespoon extra-virgin olive oil
- 1/3 cup prepared pesto
- 1 cup halved cherry tomatoes
- 1/4 teaspoon ground pepper
- 2 tablespoons balsamic vinegar
- 4 cups arugula
- 1/2 teaspoon salt
- 1 avocado, diced
- 2 cups cooked quinoa

Instructions:

1. Whisk salt, pesto, oil, pepper, and vinegar in a bowl. Measure 4 tablespoons of the mixture and put them in a bowl. Set aside.
2. Place a skillet on medium-high heat. Add the shrimp and cook for 5 minutes. The shrimp should appear slightly charred by then. Put the shrimp on a plate.
3. Add quinoa and arugula to the bowl that contains the vinaigrette. Toss to coat. Share the quinoa mixture in 4 bowls.
4. Top with the shrimp, tomatoes, and avocado. In each bowl, drizzle a tablespoon of the pesto mixture you reserved earlier.
5. Serve and enjoy!

Colorful Mixed Salad

 Servings: 2   Total Time: 25 minutes

This is a combo with many ingredients, all of which contribute to healthy blood pressure in one way or another. This salad lowers blood sugar levels, further contributing to a healthy blood circulatory system.

Nutritional Facts

369 calories   51 g carbohydrates
14 g proteins   14 g fats

Ingredients:

- 1/2 cup cherry tomatoes, finely chopped
- 1 large English cucumber, finely diced
- 1/2 cup cooked French green lentils
- 2/3 cup cooked corn kernels, thawed if frozen
- 1 small green or red bell pepper, finely diced
- 1/3 cup unsalted roasted peanuts
- 2 tablespoons coriander chutney
- 1 cup puffed quinoa
- 1/3 cup finely chopped red onion
- 1/4 cup tamarind-date chutney
- 1/4 cup finely chopped fresh cilantro

Instructions:

1. Share the corn, cucumber, lentils, quinoa, and bell pepper between two bowls.
2. Drizzle the coriander and tamarind-date chutneys over the ingredients in both bowls.
3. Top with cilantro, tomatoes, peanuts, and onion.
4. Serve and enjoy!

White Bean Soup

 Servings: 8   Total Time: 2 hours 30 minutes (30 minutes cooking time)

Help your blood vessels relax by eating this bean soup. Relaxed vessels enhance unpressured blood circulation.

Nutritional Facts

256 calories   42 g carbohydrates
13 g proteins   5 g fats

Ingredients:

- 2 large onions, finely chopped
- 1 pound dried white beans, soaked overnight
- 1 quart water
- 2 large carrots, finely chopped
- 2 tablespoons extra-virgin olive oil
- 2 large ripe tomatoes, peeled and mashed, or 1 tablespoon tomato paste
- 2 stalks celery, finely chopped
- ⅛ teaspoon cayenne pepper
- 2 teaspoons dried oregano
- Freshly ground pepper, to taste
- 1 teaspoon salt

Instructions:

1. Boil water in a large pot and cook the beans for about 1 hour until they are tender. Drain the water off.
2. Put oil in a soup pot over medium heat.
3. Saute the carrots, onions, and celery for no more than 5 minutes.
4. Add oregano, pepper, cooked beans, cayenne, tomatoes, and salt into the pot. Cook for about 20 minutes.
5. Serve and enjoy!

Seitan BBQ Sandwiches

 Servings: 4   Total Time: 25 minutes

Seitan doesn't contain sodium, which makes it perfect for hypertension patients. It's also rich in calcium and protein, making it an excellent substitute for fatty meats.

Nutritional Facts

304 calories   38 g carbohydrates
14 g proteins   11 g fats

Ingredients:

- 1/2 teaspoon ground pepper
- 1 tablespoon brown sugar
- 1/4 cup no-salt-added ketchup
- 2 teaspoons garlic powder
- 2 tablespoons cider vinegar
- 4 whole-wheat hamburger buns, split and toasted
- 1 1/2 cups very thinly sliced cabbage
- 1 tablespoon vegan Worcestershire sauce
- 1 8-ounce package seitan, sliced
- 2 tablespoons vegan mayonnaise
- 8 pickles
- 1 tablespoon canola oil

Instructions:

1. Whisk brown sugar, pepper, vinegar, and Worcestershire, garlic powder in a bowl.
2. In another bowl, mix mayonnaise and cabbage.
3. Put oil in a saucepan and heat it before adding seitan. Cook the seitan for about 6 minutes until it appears brownish. Add the ketchup mixture and continue cooking for 3 more minutes.
4. Remove the saucepan from the heat and share the mixture between the buns. Top with pickles and the cabbage mixture.
5. Serve and enjoy!

Chicken and Beet Salad

 Servings: 4   Total Time: 15 minutes

Beets are a rich source of nitrates. These nitrates are converted into nitric oxide inside your body. Nitric oxide relaxes your blood vessels, making it easy for blood to flow with less pressure.

Nutritional Facts

380 calories   15 g carbohydrates
24 g proteins   25 g fats

Ingredients:

- 3/4 cup shaved Brussels sprouts
- 1 tablespoon white balsamic vinegar
- 1/4 cup extra-virgin olive oil
- 1/4 teaspoon ground pepper
- 2 tablespoons tart cherry juice concentrate
- 1/4 cup chopped walnuts, toasted
- 1 5-ounce package spring mix salad greens
- 1 teaspoon salt
- 1 8.8-ounce package cooked beets, quartered
- 1/4 teaspoon grated lime zest
- 1/2 cup crumbled goat cheese
- 2 1/2 cups chopped or shredded cooked chicken breast

Instructions:

1. Add vinegar, lime zest, oil, pepper, juice concentrate, and salt into a bowl. Whisk the ingredients.
2. Add the Brussels sprouts, chicken, salad greens, and beets. Toss to coat.
3. Share the salad between four plates. Top with walnuts.
4. Serve and enjoy!

Tangy Chicken Salad With Grapes

 Servings: 6   Total Time: 10 minutes

Here is another way to prepare your chicken and take care of your blood pressure levels. Grapes are rich in vitamin C and antioxidants that are good for your heart system.

Nutritional Facts

350 calories	7 g carbohydrates
37 g proteins	19 g fats

Ingredients:

- 1 tablespoon fresh lemon juice
- 1/2 cup canola mayonnaise
- 1/2 teaspoon black pepper
- 1/2 cup plain whole-milk Greek yogurt
- 1/2 cup diced celery
- 2 teaspoons Dijon mustard
- 1/4 cup sliced scallions, divided
- 5 cups chopped rotisserie chicken breast
- 1 head butter lettuce
- 1 cup halved red seedless grapes

Instructions:

1. Add the lemon juice, pepper, mayonnaise, Dijon, and yogurt into a bowl. Stir well to mix.
2. Add celery, chicken, grapes, and 3 tablespoons of scallions. Toss well.
3. Put the mixture on butter lettuce leaves. Add the remaining scallions as a topping.
4. Serve and enjoy.

Southwest Chopped Salad With Tomatillo Dressing

 Servings: 4   Total Time: 25 minutes

The tomatillo dressing can lower your blood pressure. It can also help reduce weight, further improving cardiovascular health.

Nutritional Facts

519 calories   37 g carbohydrates
15 g proteins   37 g fats

Ingredients:

- 2 small cloves garlic, crushed and peeled
- 1/2 cup diced tomatillos
- 1/3 cup extra-virgin olive oil
- 1/2 cup fresh cilantro leaves
- 1 cup small grape tomatoes, halved
- 1 tablespoon lime juice
- 1 tablespoon finely chopped seeded jalapeño pepper
- 1 1/4 cups thinly sliced, slender multicolored carrots
- 3/4 teaspoon kosher salt
- 2 tablespoons distilled white vinegar
- 4 cups chopped red cabbage
- 2 teaspoons agave syrup
- 1 medium yellow bell pepper, diced
- 1/4 teaspoon ground cumin
- 1 ripe avocado, diced
- 1 15-ounce can no-salt-added red beans, rinsed
- 1 cup diced peeled jicama
- 1 cup diced pepper Jack cheese

Instructions:

1. Add garlic, lime juice, tomatillos, jalapeño, agave, oil, cilantro, cumin, salt, and vinegar into a blender. Pulse until the ingredients are smooth.
2. Combine beans, cabbage, jicama, cheese, carrots, tomatoes, and bell pepper in a bowl. Also, add the dressing and then toss the ingredients together.
3. Scatter avocado pieces on top.
4. Serve and enjoy!

Red Beans and Rice With Chicken

 Servings: 4   Total Time: 20 minutes

The red beans are rich in potassium, which improves blood pressure levels. The beans also have fiber, which remarkably reduces cholesterol levels, further contributing to a healthier cardiovascular system.

Nutritional Facts

272 calories	30 g carbohydrates
25 g proteins	5 g fats

Ingredients:

- 10 ounces skinless, boneless chicken breast, cut into 1-inch pieces
- 2 cloves garlic, minced
- 1 tablespoon olive oil
- 1/4 teaspoon salt
- 1/4 teaspoon cayenne pepper
- 1/2 cup chopped onion (1 medium)
- 1/4 teaspoon ground black pepper
- 1 15-ounce can no-salt-added red beans, rinsed and drained
- 3/4 cup green sweet pepper, coarsely chopped
- 1/4 cup reduced-sodium chicken broth
- 1 container ready-to-serve cooked brown rice
- Lime wedges
- 1/2 teaspoon ground cumin
- 1 pinch cayenne pepper

Instructions:

1. Sprinkle black pepper and salt over the chicken.
2. Add oil to a skillet over medium-high heat.
3. Add the onion, chicken, garlic, and sweet pepper to the chicken. Cook for 10 minutes while stirring. The chicken should lose its original pink color.
4. Add the rice, beans, broth, and cayenne pepper to the skillet. Stir well. Heat the mixture before serving with lime wedges.
5. Enjoy!

Mushroom and Tofu Stir-Fry

 Servings: 5

 Total Time: 20 minutes

You can never go wrong with the mushroom-tofu combo if you want to keep your blood pressure in check. Mushrooms are low in sodium, while tofu has an amino acid called tyramine, which controls blood pressure levels.

Nutritional Facts

171 calories   9 g carbohydrates
8 g proteins   13 g fats

Ingredients:

- ☼ 1 large clove garlic, grated
- ☼ 1 medium red bell pepper, diced
- ☼ 4 tablespoons peanut oil or canola oil, divided
- ☼ 1 tablespoon grated fresh ginger
- ☼ 1 pound mixed mushrooms, sliced
- ☼ 3 tablespoons oyster sauce or vegetarian oyster sauce
- ☼ 1 8-ounce container baked tofu or smoked tofu, diced
- ☼ 1 bunch scallions, trimmed and cut into 2-inch pieces

Instructions:

1. Add 2 tablespoons oil to a skillet. Place it over high heat.
2. Add bell pepper and mushrooms. Cook for about 4 minutes.
3. Add ginger, garlic, and scallions. Stir well to combine the ingredients and cook for 30 more seconds.
4. Put the cooked vegetables into a bowl and set aside.
5. Put the remaining oil into the skillet and then add tofu. Cook for 2 minutes and turn before continuing for 2 more minutes.
6. Add the oyster sauces and vegetables. Stir well. Cook for a minute while stirring.
7. Serve and enjoy!

Strawberry Spinach Salad With Avocado and Walnuts

 Servings: 1   Total Time: 5 minutes

It's not that your body doesn't need fats; it requires healthy ones such as those found in walnuts and avocados. These two are great sources of omega-3 fatty acids, which help to keep bad cholesterol levels in check. This helps to control your blood pressure.

Nutritional Facts

296 calories   27 g carbohydrates
8 g proteins   18 g fats

Ingredients:

- 2 tablespoons vinaigrette
- 1/2 cup sliced strawberries
- 3 cups baby spinach
- 1/4 medium avocado, diced
- 1 tablespoon finely chopped red onion
- 2 tablespoons toasted walnut pieces

Instructions:

1. Combine strawberries, spinach, and onion in a bowl.
2. Drizzle the vinaigrette over the salad. Toss to coat before topping with walnuts and avocado.
3. Serve and enjoy!

Rainbow Grain Bowl With Cashew Sauce

 Servings: 1   Total Time: 20 minutes

The bright colors in this recipe are not just to appetize you. They represent the variety of nutrients the meal has, some of which benefit your heart system.

Nutritional Facts

361 calories   54 g carbohydrates
17 g proteins   10 g fats

Ingredients:

- 1/2 teaspoon reduced-sodium tamari
- 1/4 cup packed parsley leaves
- 3/4 cup unsalted cashews
- 1/4 cup sliced cucumber
- 1 tablespoon extra-virgin olive oil
- 1/2 cup water
- 2 tablespoons cashew sauce
- 1/4 cup grated raw beet
- 1/4 teaspoon salt
- 1 tablespoon lemon juice
- 1/2 cup shredded red cabbage
- 1/2 cup cooked lentils
- 1/4 cup chopped bell pepper
- 1/2 cup cooked quinoa
- 1 tablespoon chopped and toasted cashews for garnish
- 1/4 cup grated carrot

Instructions:

1. Add lemon juice, tamari, cashews, parsley, oil, salt, and water into a blender. Process until the ingredients are smooth.
2. Put quinoa and lentils at the center of a serving bowl. Top with carrot, cabbage, cucumber, pepper, and beet. Add the cashew sauces and garnish with cashews.
3. Serve and enjoy!

Shrimp Paella

 Servings: 4   Total Time: 20 minutes

You don't want to miss the heart-benefiting effects of the ingredients in this recipe. The fiber, omega-3 fatty acid, and antioxidant combo will give you an edge over high blood pressure.

Nutritional Facts

336 calories	44 g carbohydrates
19 g proteins	11 g fats

Ingredients:

- 2 (8.8-oz.) pkg. precooked brown rice
- 1 cup chopped red bell pepper
- 2 tablespoons canola oil
- 2 tablespoons fresh lemon juice
- 1 tablespoon minced garlic
- 1 cup chopped red bell pepper
- 3 tablespoons unsalted chicken stock
- 1 cup frozen green peas
- 12 ounces frozen medium shrimp, thawed, peeled, and deveined
- 3/4 teaspoon kosher salt
- 1/2 teaspoon black pepper

Instructions:

1. Add the oil to a skillet and place it over medium-high.
2. Add garlic, bell pepper, and peas. Cook for 2 more minutes while stirring occasionally.
3. Add rice to the skillet and spread it in one layer. Cook for about 10 minutes without stirring.
4. Lower the heat to medium before adding the stock, pepper, and salt. Stir.
5. Evenly spread the rice mixture in the skillet to form a layer. Cook for 7 more minutes without stirring.
6. Carefully arrange the shrimp on top of the rice mixture layer. Cook for about 4 minutes.
7. Drizzle the lemon juice over the skillet contents.
8. Serve and enjoy!

Walnut-Rosemary-Crusted Salmon

 Servings: 4   Total Time: 20 minutes

Did you know that rosemary has similar effects to medications that reduce blood pressure? Well, combining this herb with salmon and walnuts will yield even better results.

Nutritional Facts

222 calories	4 g carbohydrates
24 g proteins	12 g fats

Ingredients:

- 2 teaspoons Dijon mustard
- 1/2 teaspoon kosher salt
- 1/4 teaspoon lemon zest
- 1 teaspoon lemon juice
- 1 clove garlic, minced
- 1/2 teaspoon honey
- 1/4 teaspoon lemon zest
- 1/4 teaspoon crushed red pepper
- 1 teaspoon fresh rosemary, chopped
- 1 teaspoon extra-virgin olive oil
- 3 tablespoons panko breadcrumbs
- Olive oil cooking spray
- 3 tablespoons finely chopped walnuts
- Chopped fresh parsley and lemon wedges for garnish
- 1 1-pound skinless salmon fillet, fresh

Instructions:

1. Preheat your oven to a temperature of 425 °F.
2. Use the parchment paper to line the baking sheet.
3. Add lemon juice, garlic, honey, salt, mustard, rosemary, lemon zest, and red pepper into a bowl. Mix to combine.
4. In another bowl, add oil, panko, and walnuts.
5. Arrange the salmon on the baking sheet and spread the mustard mixture on top.
6. Sprinkle the panko mixture over the fish before coating it with the cooking spray.
7. Bake for about 12 minutes, until the salmon flakes easily.
8. Sprinkle parsley over the fish.
9. Serve along with lime wedges.
10. Enjoy!

Grilled Blackened Shrimp Tacos

 Servings: 4　　　　 Total Time: 20 minutes

Omega-3 fatty acids can effectively lower your blood pressure. Get these healthy fats in this recipe, which includes the shrimp.

Nutritional Facts

286 calories　　　30 g carbohydrates
24 g proteins　　　9 g fats

Ingredients:

- 2 cups iceberg lettuce, chopped
- 1 small clove garlic, grated
- 1 ripe avocado
- 1 pound large raw shrimp, peeled and deveined
- 1 tablespoon lime juice
- 8 corn tortillas, warmed
- 1/4 teaspoon salt
- 1/2 cup fresh cilantro leaves
- 2 tablespoons salt-free Cajun spice blend
- 1/2 cup prepared pico de gallo

Instructions:

1. Heat the grill to medium-high.
2. Put the avocado in a bowl and mash it. Add garlic, salt, and lemon juice. Mix well to combine.
3. Put the shrimp and Cajun seasoning in a bowl. Toss together.
4. Thread the shrimp on a 12-inch metal skewer. Grill the shrimp for 2 minutes. Turn it and grill for 2 more minutes.
5. Serve along with tortillas. Top with lettuce, pico de gallo, cilantro, and guacamole.
6. Enjoy!

Miso-Maple Salmon

 Servings: 8   Total Time: 15 minutes

Enjoy your lunch with this blood pressure–regulating recipe. Research has shown that miso inhibits the activity of angiotensin-converting enzymes (ACE) (Ito et al., 2017). This has the effect of lowering your blood pressure to normal levels.

Nutritional Facts

230 calories   7 g carbohydrates
28 g proteins   9 g fats

Ingredients:

- 1/4 cup white miso
- 2 lemons
- 1/4 teaspoon ground pepper
- 2 tablespoons maple syrup
- 2 limes
- Sliced scallions for garnish
- A pinch of cayenne pepper
- 2 tablespoons extra-virgin olive oil
- 1 (2 1/2-pound) skin-on salmon fillet

Instructions:

1. Make sure your rack is in the upper third of the oven, and preheat the broiler to high. Meanwhile, use foil to coat your baking pan.
2. Squeeze the juice from one lemon and one lime. Combine the juice in one bowl.
3. Add pepper, miso, maple syrup, cayenne, and oil to the bowl with the juice. Whisk to combine the ingredients.
4. Arrange the salmon in the baking pan with the skin side facing down.
5. Spread the miso mixture on top of the salmon.
6. Cut the remaining lime and lemon into halves. Arrange these halves around the salmon, with the cut sides facing upward.
7. Broil the salmon for about 12 minutes.
8. Serve along with the lime and lemon halves.
9. Enjoy!

Cabbage, Tofu, and Edamame Salad

 Servings: 1   Total Time: 10 minutes

This recipe includes cabbage, which contains anthocyanins. Research has confirmed the role of anthocyanins in lowering high blood pressure (Zhu et al., 2016).

Nutritional Facts

368 calories   44 g carbohydrates
20 g proteins   12 g fats

Ingredients:

- 1/2 cup bamboo shoots
- 3 ounces baked tofu cubes
- 4 cups mesclun
- 1/2 cup edamame
- 1/2 cup shredded red cabbage
- 1 tablespoon golden raisins
- 1/2 cup grated carrots
- 2 tablespoons chow mein noodles
- 1/4 cup mandarin oranges
- 2 tablespoons bottled reduced-sugar Asian sesame vinaigrette

Instructions:

1. Mix tofu, oranges, carrots, mesclun, bamboo shoots, edamame, chow mein noodles, cabbage, and raisins in a bowl.
2. Drizzle the vinaigrette over the ingredients.
3. Serve and enjoy!

Baked Fish Tacos With Avocado

 Servings: 4   Total Time: 20 minutes

This recipe is rich in omega-3 fatty acids from the avocado and fish. By taking charge of the cholesterol levels in your body, you also address blood pressure issues.

Nutritional Facts

460 calories   53 g carbohydrates
29 g proteins   17 g fats

Ingredients:

- 1/2 cup pico de gallo
- 1/2 teaspoon salt
- 1 tablespoon avocado oil
- 1 avocado, cut into 16 slices
- 2 teaspoons no-salt-added Mexican-style seasoning blend
- 8 corn tortillas, warmed
- 1 pound flaky white fish fillets

Instructions:

1. Preheat your oven to a temperature of 400 °F.
2. Use cooking spray to coat the baking sheet.
3. Add salt, oil, and the seasoning blend to a bowl. Stir to combine before adding fish. Toss to coat. Spread the mixture on the baking sheet and bake for about 10 minutes. The fish should end up flaking easily.
4. Top each tortilla with 2 avocado slices, a piece of fish, and a tablespoon of pico de gallo.
5. Fold in, serve, and enjoy!

Chickpea Pasta With Mushrooms and Kale

 Servings: 4   Total Time: 30 minutes

This is a protein-rich recipe that will help regulate your blood pressure. Mushrooms are naturally low in sodium, so they can maintain normal blood pressure levels.

Nutritional Facts

340 calories   38 g carbohydrates
17 g proteins   18 g fats

Ingredients:

- 8 ounces chickpea rotini
- 8 cups chopped kale
- A pinch of crushed red pepper
- 1/4 cup extra-virgin olive oil
- 1/2 teaspoon salt
- 8 ounces cremini mushrooms, quartered
- 2 large cloves garlic, sliced
- 1/2 teaspoon dried thyme

Instructions:

1. Cook the pasta based on the instructions on the package. Get a cup of pasta water and set it aside. Drain the pasta.
2. Add oil to a skillet and place it on medium heat. Add the pepper and garlic. Cook for about a minute while stirring.
3. Add thyme, kale, salt, and mushrooms. Cook for about 5 minutes while stirring occasionally.
4. Add the pasta, along with the water that you reserved earlier. Only put the water in enough to coat it. Cook for another minute.
5. Serve and enjoy!

Classic Sesame Noodles With Chicken

 Servings: 4   Total Time: 20 minutes

Sesame products are a good addition to your diet, considering that they are rich in potassium. This mineral dilates your blood vessels, thereby lowering blood pressure.

Nutritional Facts

460 calories   53 g carbohydrates
29 g proteins   17 g fats

Ingredients:

- 1 teaspoon brown sugar
- 3 tablespoons toasted sesame seeds
- 2 scallions, chopped
- 8 ounces whole-wheat spaghetti
- 8 ounces cooked boneless, skinless chicken breast, shredded
- 2 teaspoons minced fresh ginger
- 3 tablespoons toasted (dark) sesame oil
- 2 tablespoons reduced-sodium soy sauce
- 1 tablespoon minced garlic
- 1 cup julienned carrots
- 2 tablespoons ketchup
- 1 cup sliced snap peas

Instructions:

1. Cook the spaghetti as directed in the package instructions. Drain and rinse the spaghetti before putting it in a bowl.
2. Combine garlic, brown sugar, sesame oil, ginger, and scallions in a saucepan. Put the saucepan on medium heat until the ingredients begin to sizzle. Cook for about 15 seconds before removing the heat. Add the ketchup and soy sauce. Stir well.
3. Add the saucepan contents to the noodle bowl. Also, add carrots, sesame seeds, and snap peas. Toss to combine the ingredients.
4. Enjoy!

Bean Salad With Lemon-Cumin Dressing

 Servings: 10   Total Time: 25 minutes

This is more than just a bean salad; it is coupled with lemon-cumin dressing. Both cumin and lemon help to keep your blood pressure in check.

Nutritional Facts

221 calories   22 g carbohydrates
6 g proteins   12 g fats

Ingredients:

- 1/2 cup chopped fresh mint
- 1/2 cup extra-virgin olive oil
- 1 small clove garlic, chopped
- 1 15-ounce can chickpeas, rinsed
- 2 tablespoons ground cumin
- 1 teaspoon kosher salt, divided
- 2 15-ounce cans dark-red kidney beans, rinsed
- 1/4 cup lemon juice
- 1 cup carrot, finely diced
- 1/4 teaspoon ground cinnamon
- 1 1/2 cups fresh parsley, chopped

Instructions:

1. Add 1/2 teaspoon salt and garlic in a bowl. Mash the garlic to form a paste.
2. Add cumin, cinnamon, oil, lemon juice, and the remaining salt. Whisk to mix the ingredients.
3. Add chickpeas, parsley, kidney beans, carrots, and mint. Stir well.
4. Serve and enjoy!

Chicken, Brussels Sprouts, and Mushroom Salad

 Servings: 4   Total Time: 10 minutes

The protein-rich chicken, low-sodium mushroom, and low-cholesterol Brussels sprouts are effective in addressing blood pressure issues.

Nutritional Facts

432 calories	15 g carbohydrates
24 g proteins	31 g fats

Ingredients:

- ☼ 4 cups packed baby arugula
- ☼ 1 1/2 tablespoons minced shallot
- ☼ 6 tablespoons olive oil
- ☼ 2 teaspoons chopped fresh thyme
- ☼ 3 tablespoons red-wine vinegar
- ☼ 12 ounces shredded cooked chicken
- ☼ 1 tablespoon Dijon mustard
- ☼ 4 cups shaved Brussels sprouts
- ☼ 1/2 teaspoon ground pepper
- ☼ 1 cup thinly diagonally sliced celery
- ☼ 4 cups shaved fresh cremini mushrooms
- ☼ 1 cup shaved Parmesan cheese

Instructions:

1. Add thyme, vinegar, pepper, oil, mustard, and shallot into a bowl and whisk.
2. Add the celery, mushrooms, arugula, Brussels sprouts, and chicken.
3. Sprinkle with Parmesan and serve.
4. Enjoy!

Loaded Black Bean Nacho Soup

 Servings: 2   Total Time: 10 minutes

Are you looking for another recipe for preparing your black beans, considering how beneficial they are in a "blood pressure" diet? If yes, look no further; try this recipe and enjoy!

Nutritional Facts

350 calories   44 g carbohydrates
10 g proteins   17 g fats

Ingredients:

- 1 18-ounce carton low-sodium black bean soup
- 1/2 medium avocado, diced
- 1/2 cup halved grape tomatoes
- 1/4 teaspoon smoked paprika
- 2 tablespoons crumbled cotija cheese or other Mexican-style shredded cheese
- 1/2 teaspoon lime juice
- 2 ounces baked tortilla chips
- 1/2 cup shredded cabbage or slaw mix

Instructions:

1. Pour the soup into a saucepan. Add paprika and stir well. Heat the soup, following the instructions on the package. Add lime juice and stir well.
2. Share the soup between 2 bowls. Top with the cabbage, avocado, tomatoes, and cheese.
3. Serve along with tortilla chips.
4. Enjoy!

Lemony Linguine With Spring Vegetables

 Servings: 4   Total Time: 30 minutes

Whole-wheat linguine helps maintain normal blood sugar levels. Making it lemony adds some antioxidants that are beneficial to your heart system.

Nutritional Facts

372 calories   64 g carbohydrates
18 g proteins   7 g fats

Ingredients:

- 8 ounces whole-wheat linguine
- 6 cups chopped mature spinach
- 1/4 teaspoon ground pepper
- 4 cloves garlic, thinly sliced
- 1/4 cup half-and-half
- 1 9-ounce package frozen artichoke hearts
- 1/2 teaspoon salt
- 2 cups peas, fresh
- 3 1/2 cups water
- 1 tablespoon lemon zest
- 1/2 cup grated Parmesan cheese, divided
- 3 tablespoons lemon juice

Instructions:

1. Add the pasta, pepper, salt, and garlic into a pot.
2. Add water and boil the ingredients over high heat for about 8 minutes. Stir continuously as you cook.
3. Add spinach, peas, and artichokes. Cook for 4 more minutes. Most of the water should have evaporated by then.
4. Remove the pot from the heat and then add the half-and-half and 1/4 cup cheese, as well as the lemon juice and zest. Stir and leave for 5 minutes.
5. Sprinkle the remaining cheese and serve.
6. Enjoy!

Crunchy Chicken and Mango Salad

 Servings: 4   Total Time: 20 minutes

Not only is this recipe healthy for your cardiovascular system, but it is also tasty. Mangoes have potassium and magnesium, both of which contribute to regulating your pulse and blood pressure.

Nutritional Facts

285 calories   25 g carbohydrates
27 g proteins   9 g fats

Ingredients:

- 6 cups thinly sliced napa cabbage
- 3 tablespoons less-sodium soy sauce
- 1/3 cup orange juice
- 1/4 cup scallions, sliced
- 3 tablespoons rice vinegar
- 2 cups sugar snap peas, thinly sliced diagonally
- 1 tablespoon toasted sesame oil
- 1/2 cup fresh mint, coarsely chopped
- 2 cups cooked chicken breast, shredded
- 2 tablespoons sesame seeds, toasted
- 1 medium mango, sliced

Instructions:

1. Whisk the soy sauce, juice, sesame oil, and vinegar in a bowl.
2. Add mango, scallions, cabbage, mint, chicken, and peas. Toss to coat.
3. Sprinkle sesame seeds over the salad.
4. Serve and enjoy!

Teriyaki Chicken Skillet Casserole With Broccoli

 Servings: 6   Total Time: 30 minutes

Broccoli harbors antioxidants that enhance the levels of nitric oxide levels in your body. This helps blood vessels to relax, a state that reduces blood pressure.

Nutritional Facts

314 calories   33 g carbohydrates
26 g proteins   8 g fats

Ingredients:

- 3 cups sliced cooked chicken
- 1 cup diced red bell pepper
- 2 tablespoons sesame oil
- 1/4 cup water
- 1/3 cup low-sodium teriyaki sauce
- 3 cups bite-size broccoli florets
- 2 tablespoons cornstarch
- 1 cup sliced scallions
- 3 cups cooked brown rice
- 2 cloves garlic, grated

Instructions:

1. Preheat your oven to a temperature of 350 °F.
2. Add oil into a skillet and place it on medium heat.
3. Add scallions, broccoli, and bell pepper to the skillet. Cook for about 5 minutes while stirring.
4. Combine cornstarch, teriyaki sauce, garlic, and water in a small bowl. Add the mixture to the skillet, along with the rice and chicken. Stir well to combine.
5. Put the skillet in the oven and bake for about 15 minutes.
6. Serve and enjoy!

Chopped Power Salad With Chicken

 Servings: 4   Total Time: 20 minutes

Here is another salad that will not only excite your taste buds but also help to keep your blood pressure in check!

Nutritional Facts

466 calories   14 g carbohydrates
49 g proteins   24 g fats

Ingredients:

- ✿ 1 clove garlic, grated
- ✿ 1/4 cup extra-virgin olive oil
- ✿ 1/3 cup crumbled feta cheese
- ✿ 1/2 teaspoon sugar
- ✿ 3 tablespoons lemon juice
- ✿ 1 cup halved and sliced cucumber
- ✿ 1/4 teaspoon ground pepper
- ✿ 1/2 teaspoon dried oregano
- ✿ 4 cups baby spinach
- ✿ 1/4 teaspoon salt
- ✿ 1 cup halved grape tomatoes
- ✿ 4 cups torn green-leaf lettuce
- ✿ 1/2 cup slivered red onion
- ✿ 2 cups shredded cooked chicken
- ✿ 2 tablespoons unsalted roasted sunflower seeds
- ✿ 1/3 cup sliced pepperoncini

Instructions:

1. Add oregano, lemon juice, pepper, garlic, salt, oil, and sugar into a bowl. Whisk to mix.
2. Add onion, chicken, lettuce, pepperoncini, cucumber, tomatoes, and spinach. Toss to coat.
3. Sprinkle sunflower seeds and feta.
4. Serve and enjoy!

DINNER RECIPES

Find the dinner recipes in this section.

Veggie and Hummus Sandwich

 Servings: 1   Total Time: 10 minutes

Carrots, greens, and cucumbers are great for heart health. For example, one study reported that daily consumption of 100 g of carrots was associated with a 10% reduction in blood pressure (Madsen et al., 2023).

Nutritional Facts

325 calories	40 g carbohydrates
13 g proteins	14 g fats

Ingredients:

- ⚙ 1/4 cup sliced cucumber
- ⚙ 1/4 avocado, mashed
- ⚙ 2 slices whole-grain bread
- ⚙ 1/4 medium red bell pepper, sliced
- ⚙ 3 tablespoons hummus
- ⚙ 1/4 cup shredded carrot
- ⚙ 1/2 cup mixed salad greens

Instructions:

1. Spread hummus on one side of one slice of bread. Spread avocado on the other slice.
2. Place the "hummus slice" with the spread side facing up. Add the cucumbers, greens, carrots, and bell pepper on top.
3. Place the "avocado slice" on the toppings, with the spread side facing down.
4. Cut the sandwich in half.
5. Serve and enjoy!

Black Bean Tacos and Roasted Vegetable

 Servings: 2   Total Time: 15 minutes

Black beans have a wealth of saponins, which are plant-based compounds that can lower cholesterol levels. The fiber in the beans also has similar effects.

Nutritional Facts

343 calories   44 g carbohydrates
8 g proteins   17 g fats

Ingredients:

- 1/2 teaspoon ground coriander
- 1 lime, cut into wedges
- 2 teaspoons extra-virgin olive oil
- 1 cup roasted root vegetables
- 1 teaspoon chili powder
- 1/2 cup cooked or canned black beans, rinsed
- 1/2 avocado, cut into 8 slices
- 1/4 teaspoon kosher salt
- 1 teaspoon ground cumin
- 1/4 teaspoon ground pepper
- 4 corn tortillas, lightly toasted or warmed

Instructions:

1. Add the oil, chili powder, pepper, cumin, root vegetables, salt, beans, and coriander in a saucepan. Cook for 8 minutes on medium-low heat while covered.
2. Divide the mixture into 4 parts and use it to top the tortillas.
3. Add avocado on top of the mixture.
4. Serve with lime wedges.
5. Enjoy!

Tex-Mex Pasta Salad

 Servings: 1   Total Time: 15 minutes

Whole-wheat pasta has healthy starches that do not cause blood sugar spikes. This reduces the need to convert excess sugars into fat for storage. Extra fat could clog your blood vessels and cause hypertension.

Nutritional Facts

403 calories   51 g carbohydrates
24 g proteins   13 g fats

Ingredients:

- 1 tablespoon tomatillo salsa
- 1/4 cup chopped red onion
- 1 tablespoon toasted pepitas
- 3/4 cup chopped red bell pepper
- 1 tablespoon low-fat plain Greek yogurt
- 1/8 teaspoon ground pepper
- 1/2 cup cooked orzo, preferably whole-wheat, cooled
- 1 cup cherry tomatoes, halved
- 2 tablespoons shredded pepper Jack cheese
- 3/4 cup frozen shelled edamame (4 oz.), cooked according to package directions, drained, and cooled
- Hot sauce, to taste
- 1/8 teaspoon salt
- Lime wedge for serving

Instructions:

1. Combine yogurt and salsa in a bowl. Whisk and set the mixture aside.
2. Add the bell pepper, onion, tomatoes, edamame, cheese, and orzo in another bowl. Mix and then add pepper, salt, and the salsa dressing. Toss to mix the ingredients.
3. Season with hot sauce before sprinkling pepitas.
4. Serve along with a lime wedge.
5. Enjoy!

Smoked Turkey, Kale, and Rice Bake

 Servings: 6   Total Time: 40 minutes

Do your cardiovascular system a favor by preparing this meal. The lean protein in turkey helps you manage your weight, ultimately giving you an edge over high blood pressure.

Nutritional Facts

266 calories   26 g carbohydrates
18 g proteins   11 g fats

Ingredients:

- 1 tablespoon extra-virgin olive oil
- 1 cup instant or quick-cooking brown rice
- 4 cups slivered kale leaves
- 2 cups thinly sliced leeks, white and light green parts only
- 1 cup low-fat, no-salt-added cottage cheese
- 1 cup thinly sliced celery
- 1 teaspoon freshly ground pepper, or to taste
- 1 1/2 cups smoked turkey breast or smoked tofu, chopped
- 1 28-ounce can diced tomatoes
- 1/4 cup water
- 1 cup shredded extra-sharp Cheddar cheese

Instructions:

1. Add oil to a skillet over medium heat.
2. Add celery and leeks. Cook while stirring consistently for about 3 minutes.
3. Add tomatoes and kale. Cook for 2 more minutes.
4. Add the turkey, cottage cheese, pepper, rice, and water.
5. Reduce the heat to medium-low and let the ingredients simmer for about 10 minutes while covered.
6. Preheat the broiler and position the rack on the upper third level of the oven.
7. With the skillet open, cook the rice mixture for 10 more minutes while uncovered. Most of the liquid should evaporate.
8. Add the cheese and broil for 3 minutes so that the cheese begins to bubble.
9. Serve enjoy!

Mason Jar Power Salad With Chickpeas and Tuna

 Servings: 1   Total Time: 5 minutes

Think of the nutrient boost that you will get by eating chickpeas and tuna. This recipe is great for addressing blood pressure issues.

Nutritional Facts

430 calories   30 g carbohydrates

26 g proteins   23 g fats

Ingredients:

- 1/2 cup rinsed canned chickpeas
- 1 2.5-ounce pouch tuna in water
- 3 cups bite-sized pieces chopped kale
- 1 carrot, peeled and shredded
- 2 tablespoons honey-mustard vinaigrette

Instructions:

1. Combine kale and the dressing in a bowl.
2. Transfer the mixture to a 1-quart mason jar.
3. Top with carrots, tuna, and chickpeas. Close the jar and put it in the fridge for 2 days.
4. Put the jar's ingredients into a bowl. Add the dressed kale and toss.
5. Serve and enjoy!

Cream of Turkey and Wild Rice Soup

 Servings: 4

 Total Time: 35 minutes

Turkey is one of the healthy sources of lean protein that you can include in your diet. Lean protein helps you to effectively manage your weight, which is good for cardiovascular health.

Nutritional Facts

378 calories
37 g proteins

29 g carbohydrates
11 g fats

Ingredients:

- ☼ 1 tablespoon extra-virgin olive oil
- ☼ 3/4 cup chopped carrots
- ☼ 2 cups sliced mushrooms
- ☼ 1/4 teaspoon salt
- ☼ 1/4 cup all-purpose flour
- ☼ 3/4 cup chopped celery
- ☼ 1/4 teaspoon freshly ground pepper
- ☼ 1/4 cup chopped shallots
- ☼ 3 cups shredded cooked turkey
- ☼ 4 cups reduced-sodium chicken broth
- ☼ 1/2 cup reduced-fat sour cream
- ☼ 2 tablespoons chopped fresh parsley
- ☼ 1 cup quick-cooking or instant wild rice

Instructions:

1. Put a saucepan on medium heat and add oil.
2. Add the shallots, celery, mushrooms, and carrots. Cook for about 5 minutes while stirring.
3. Add flour, salt, and pepper. Cook for 2 more minutes while stirring.
4. Add broth to the saucepan and bring the ingredients to a boil.
5. Add the rice and lower the heat. Cover the saucepan and cook the rice for around 7 minutes.
6. Add the sour cream, turkey, and parsley. Stir well to combine. Cook for 2 minutes until the turkey is heated through.
7. Serve and enjoy!

Slow-Cooker Chicken and White Bean Stew

 Servings: 1   ⏱ Total Time: 7 hours 45 minutes (10 minutes active time)

The magnesium in white beans and the protein in chicken contribute to lowering high blood pressure. Proteins are broken into peptides, some of which have the effect of reducing hypertension.

Nutritional Facts

493 calories   54 g carbohydrates
44 g proteins   11 g fats

Ingredients:

- 1 pound dried cannellini beans, soaked overnight and drained
- 1 tablespoon lemon juice
- 1 cup sliced carrots
- 6 cups unsalted chicken broth
- 1 4-ounce Parmesan cheese rind plus 2/3 cup grated Parmesan, divided
- 1 cup chopped yellow onion
- 2 tablespoons extra-virgin olive oil
- 4 cups chopped kale
- 1 teaspoon fresh rosemary, finely chopped
- 1/2 teaspoon kosher salt
- 2 1-pound bone-in chicken breasts
- 1/2 cup flat-leaf parsley leaves
- 1/2 teaspoon ground pepper

Instructions:

1. Add the carrots, beans, Parmesan, onions, rosemary, and broth to a slow cooker. Add the chicken, cover, and cook on Low for about 7 hours.
2. Take the chicken out of the slow cooker and place it on a cutting board. Let it stand for about 10 minutes so that it cools down. Shred the chicken and remove any bones.
3. Put the shredded chicken in the slow cooker, along with kale. Cover and cook for about 30 minutes.
4. Add pepper, lemon juice, and salt. Stir well before discarding the Parmesan rind.
5. Drizzle some oil over the stew. Sprinkle parsley and Parmesan before serving.
6. Enjoy!

Salmon Couscous Salad

 Servings: 1   Total Time: 10 minutes

Take control of the cholesterol balance in your blood by eating this salmon-based recipe. Remember, salmon has omega-3 fatty acids that help raise good cholesterol levels in your body.

Nutritional Facts

464 calories   35 g carbohydrates
35 g proteins   22 g fats

Ingredients:

- 4 ounces cooked salmon
- 3 cups baby spinach
- 1/4 cup sliced cremini mushrooms
- 1/4 cup cooked Israeli couscous, preferably whole-wheat
- 1/4 cup diced eggplant
- 1/4 cup sliced dried apricots
- 2 tablespoons white-wine vinaigrette, divided
- 2 tablespoons crumbled goat cheese (1/2 ounce)

Instructions:

1. Use cooking spray to coat a skillet and place it over mhigh-blood vegetables.
2. Enjoy!

Pan-Seared Steak With Crispy Herbs and Escarole

 Servings: 4   Total Time: 20 minutes

Including lean meat in your high-blood pressure diet is a great idea. The proteins in the meat aid weight management, which is crucial for controlling your blood pressure.

Nutritional Facts

244 calories   10 g carbohydrates
26 g proteins   12 g fats

Ingredients:

- 1 pound sirloin steak
- 4 cloves garlic, crushed
- 2 tablespoons grapeseed oil
- 1/2 teaspoon salt, divided
- 3 sprigs fresh sage
- 5 sprigs fresh thyme
- 1/2 teaspoon ground pepper, divided
- 16 cups chopped escarole
- 1 sprig fresh rosemary

Instructions:

1. Sprinkle a 1/4 teaspoon each of pepper and salt on the steak. Meanwhile, place a skillet over medium-high heat.
2. Add the steak to the skillet and cook for about 3 minutes. The steak should appear charred on one side.
3. Flip the steak before adding sage, garlic, rosemary, and oil. Cook while stirring for about 3 minutes.
4. Remove the steak from the skillet and put it on a plate. Top it with herbs and garlic. Cover with foil.
5. Add the remaining pepper and salt to the skillet, along with escarole. Cook for 2 minutes.
6. Cut the steak into thin slices. Serve with the crispy herbs and escarole.
7. Enjoy!

Marinara Meat Sauce–Topped Baked Potato

 Servings: 1   Total Time: 15 minutes

Potatoes are excellent sources of anthocyanins, potassium, and chlorogenic acid. These components are effective in lowering high blood pressure.

Nutritional Facts

294 calories   43 g carbohydrates
20 g proteins   5 g fats

Ingredients:

- 1 6-ounce russet potato, baked
- 3 tablespoons light pasta sauce, such as Heart Smart
- 2 ounces lean ground beef
- 1 tablespoon grated Parmesan cheese
- 1/3 cup sliced mushrooms

Instructions:

1. Cook the mushrooms and beef in a skillet. Stir occasionally as you cook.
2. Drain before adding the tomato sauce.
3. Top the potato with the Parmesan cheese and meat sauce.
4. Enjoy!

Chickpea and Quinoa Grain Bowl

 Servings: 1

 Total Time: 15 minutes

Eating chickpeas raises potassium levels in your body, thereby improving blood pressure levels. The fiber in this recipe reduces the levels of harmful cholesterol.

Nutritional Facts

503 calories   75 g carbohydrates
18 g proteins   17 g fats

Ingredients:

- 1 cup cooked quinoa
- A pinch of ground pepper
- 1 tablespoon finely chopped roasted red pepper
- 1/2 cup cherry tomatoes, halved
- 1/3 cup canned chickpeas, rinsed and drained
- 3 tablespoons hummus
- 1/2 cup cucumber slices
- 1 tablespoon lemon juice
- 1/4 avocado, diced
- A pinch of salt
- 1 tablespoon water, plus more if desired

Instructions:

1. Arrange the cucumber, quinoa, avocado, tomatoes, and chickpeas in a bowl.
2. Add the lemon juice, hummus, water, and roasted red pepper in a bowl. Stir to mix. You can adjust the consistency of the dressing by adding water. Add pepper, parsley, and salt to the dressing. Stir well.
3. Serve alongside the grain bowl.
4. Enjoy!

Hearty Tomato Soup With Beans and Greens

 Servings: 4   Total Time: 10 minutes

When you get your soup, be sure to purchase one that is low on sodium, as this supports your goals to regulate your blood pressure.

Nutritional Facts

200 calories   29 g carbohydrates
9 g proteins   6 g fats

Ingredients:

- 2 14-ounce cans low-sodium hearty-style tomato soup
- 1 teaspoon minced garlic
- 1 tablespoon olive oil
- 1 14-ounce can no-salt-added cannellini beans, rinsed
- 3 cups chopped kale
- 1/4 cup grated Parmesan cheese

Instructions:

1. Prepare the tomato soup according to the instructions on the package. Let the soup simmer on low heat.
2. Put a skillet on medium heat and add oil. Add kale and let it cook for about 2 minutes. Add garlic and cook for 30 seconds more. Stir well before adding the beans and greens to the soup. Simmer for 3 minutes.
3. Share the soup into 4 bowls. Top with Parmesan and serve.
4. Enjoy!

Saucy Ginger-Tomato Chicken

 Servings: 4   Total Time: 25 minutes

Take advantage of the potassium-rich tomatoes and keep high blood pressure at bay. Did you also know that ginger acts as an angiotensin-converting enzyme (ACE), which can treat hypertension (Vinmec International Hospital, n.d.)?

Nutritional Facts

426 calories   45 g carbohydrates
31 g proteins   13 g fats

Ingredients:

- 1 tablespoon avocado oil
- 1 tablespoon curry powder
- 1 1-inch knob fresh ginger, finely chopped
- 2 medium onions, finely chopped
- 12 ounces boneless, skinless chicken breast, cut into bite-size pieces
- 6 cloves garlic, chopped
- 1 tablespoon garam masala
- 1 11-ounce can condensed tomato soup
- 2 cups cooked brown basmati rice
- 1/4 cup heavy cream

Instructions:

1. Put oil in a saucepan over medium heat.
2. Add the ginger, garlic, and onion. Cook for about 5 minutes, while stirring.
3. Add garam masala, chicken, soup, and curry powder. Cook for 10 more minutes until the chicken is well cooked.
4. Add the cream and stir well.
5. Serve along with rice.
6. Enjoy!

Broccoli Mac and Cheese With Rotisserie Chicken

 Servings: 2   Total Time: 20 minutes

The antioxidants and flavonoids in broccoli improve the functioning ability of your blood vessels. These compounds also increase the availability of nitric oxide in your body. Nitric oxide is a vasodilator—it relaxes your blood vessels, thereby reducing the pressure of blood flow.

Nutritional Facts

408 calories	42 g carbohydrates
41 g proteins	11 g fats

Ingredients:

- ☼ 1 cup shredded rotisserie chicken
- ☼ 2 cups cooked broccoli florets
- ☼ 1 5.5-ounce box chickpea macaroni and cheese
- ☼ Cracked black pepper for serving

Instructions:

1. To prepare the macaroni and cheese, follow the instructions on the package.
2. Add the chicken and broccoli. Stir well.
3. Top with cracked pepper and serve.
4. Enjoy!

Tomato, Cucumber, and White Bean Salad With Basil Vinaigrette

 Servings: 4   Total Time: 25 minutes

Tomatoes and cucumber are both good sources of dietary potassium. White beans have good amounts of magnesium. Both potassium and magnesium are handy in lowering high blood pressure.

Nutritional Facts

246 calories   22 g carbohydrates
8 g proteins   15 g fats

Ingredients:

- 1 teaspoon honey
- 3 tablespoons red-wine vinegar
- 1/2 cup packed fresh basil leaves
- 1 cup halved cherry or grape tomatoes
- 2 teaspoons Dijon mustard
- 1/4 cup extra-virgin olive oil
- 1/4 teaspoon salt
- 1 tablespoon finely chopped shallot
- 1 (15-ounce) can low-sodium cannellini beans, rinsed
- 1/4 teaspoon ground pepper
- 1/2 cucumber, halved lengthwise and sliced
- 10 cups mixed salad greens

Instructions:

1. Add mustard, pepper, basil, honey, vinegar, salt, shallot, and oil into a food processor. Pulse until the ingredients are a smooth mixture. Transfer to a bowl.
2. Add tomatoes, greens, cucumber, and beans. Toss well to coat.
3. Serve and enjoy!

No-Cook Black Bean Salad

 Servings: 4   Total Time: 30 minutes

Take advantage of the fiber and antioxidants in black beans and reduce blood cholesterol. This helps much in preventing hypertension and maintaining a healthy cardiovascular system.

Nutritional Facts

322 calories   41 g carbohydrates
11 g proteins   16 g fats

Ingredients:

- 1/2 cup thinly sliced red onion
- 2 tablespoons extra-virgin olive oil
- 1/4 cup lime juice
- 1 medium ripe avocado, pitted and roughly chopped
- 1 pint grape tomatoes, halved
- 1 clove garlic, minced
- 1/4 cup cilantro leaves
- 2 medium ears corn, kernels removed
- 1/2 teaspoon salt
- 1 15-ounce can black beans, rinsed
- 8 cups mixed salad greens

Instructions:

1. Put the onion in a bowl and add water until just submerged. Set aside.
2. Add juice, salt, avocado, oil, cilantro, and lime juice into a food processor. Pulse until the ingredients appear smooth and creamy. This is your dressing.
3. Add tomatoes, salad greens, beans, and corn in a bowl. Drain the onions and add them to the salad bowl. Also, add the salad dressing. Toss.
4. Serve and enjoy!

Mixed Greens With Sliced Apple and Lentils

 Servings: 1   Total Time: 10 minutes

Legumes demonstrate the ability to regulate blood pressure. Fortunately enough, this recipe includes lentils, along with other greens that are beneficial to the heart system.

Nutritional Facts

347 calories   48 g carbohydrates
13 g proteins   13 g fats

Ingredients:

- ☼ 1 1/2 cups mixed salad greens
- ☼ 1 tablespoon red-wine vinegar
- ☼ 1 1/2 tablespoons crumbled feta cheese
- ☼ 1/2 cup cooked lentils
- ☼ 2 teaspoons extra-virgin olive oil
- ☼ 1 apple, cored and sliced, divided

Instructions:

1. Add the lentils and feta on top of the greens. Also, add half of the apple slices.
2. Drizzle oil and vinegar over the toppings.
3. Serve the mixed greens together with the sliced apples.
4. Enjoy!

Italian Zucchini–Topped Baked Potato

 Servings: 1   Total Time: 25 minutes

Zucchini can regulate your blood pressure in two ways. First, it has good amounts of fiber, which significantly reduces total cholesterol levels. Second, zucchini is a good source of potassium.

Nutritional Facts

281 calories   42 g carbohydrates
12 g proteins   7 g fats

Ingredients:

- 1/2 teaspoon Italian seasoning, crushed
- 1/4 cup canned no-salt-added diced tomatoes, undrained
- Nonstick cooking spray
- 1 6-ounce russet potato, baked
- 1/4 cup shredded Italian-blend cheese (1 ounce)
- 1/4 cup chopped zucchini

Instructions:

1. Use cooking spray to coat a skillet.
2. Add the tomatoes, zucchini, and Italian seasoning. Cook over medium heat for 8 minutes.
3. Add cheese and stir well.
4. Serve the potato and top with the zucchini mixture.
5. Enjoy!

Lemon-Garlic Vegetable Soup

 Servings: 41 Total Time: 40 minutes

Were you aware that garlic contains sulfur that is used to make hydrogen sulfide and nitric oxide gases? These gases help to relax your blood vessels so that blood flows with less pressure.

Nutritional Facts

347 calories   48 g carbohydrates
13 g proteins   13 g fats

Ingredients:

- 2 ears corn, kernels cut from the cob
- 1 small onion, chopped
- 4 large cloves garlic, minced
- 2 tablespoons extra-virgin olive oil
- 2 medium tomatoes, diced
- 1 medium zucchini, diced
- 1 small onion, chopped
- 4 cups low-sodium vegetable broth
- 2 cups halved green beans
- 4 teaspoons lemon juice, plus more to taste
- 1/2 teaspoon salt
- 3 cups chopped stemmed kale
- 1/4 cup chopped fresh herbs, such as basil, cilantro, tarragon or parsley
- 1/4 teaspoon ground pepper

Instructions:

1. Add oil into a pot over medium heat.
2. Add the onion and cook for about 2 minutes while stirring.
3. Add garlic and continue cooking for about 30 seconds.
4. Add corn, beans, and zucchini. Cook for 2 more minutes.
5. Add tomatoes, broth, pepper, kale, and salt into the pot. With the heat on high, bring the ingredients to a boil.
6. Reduce the heat so that the ingredients simmer for around 15 minutes.
7. Take the pot off the heat before adding the herbs and lemon juice.
8. Mix well and serve.
9. Enjoy!

Southwestern Salad With Black Beans

 Servings: 41   Total Time: 20 minutes

The greens, tomatoes, and black beans in this recipe are great for your cardiovascular system. The compounds in these ingredients can help alleviate hypertension.

Nutritional Facts

235 calories   44 g carbohydrates
13 g proteins   4 g fats

Ingredients:

- 1 tablespoon lime juice
- 1/2 cup nonfat plain yogurt
- 1/2 ripe avocado
- 1/2 cup corn kernels, fresh or frozen (thawed)
- 1 clove garlic, quartered
- 3/4 cup packed fresh cilantro
- 1/2 teaspoon sugar
- 2 scallions, chopped
- 1/2 cup black beans, canned (rinsed) or cooked
- 1/2 teaspoon salt
- 1/2 cup grape tomatoes
- 3 cups mixed greens

Instructions:

1. Add lime juice, avocado, salt, sugar, yogurt, garlic, and cilantro into a blender. Process until you get a smooth mixture.
2. Put the greens in a bowl and add 2 tablespoons of the dressing. Toss.
3. Top with tomatoes, scallions, black beans, and corn.
4. Serve and enjoy!

Eat-the-Rainbow Vegetable Soup

 Servings: 3   Total Time: 20 minutes

The different colors of the vegetables in this soup represent the wide variety of nutrients you will get by eating it. It's a great soup for keeping your blood pressure in check.

Nutritional Facts

181 calories   36 g carbohydrates
10 g proteins   1 g fats

Ingredients:

- 1 cup packed chopped spinach
- 3/4 teaspoon crushed red pepper, divided
- 1 cup matchstick carrots
- 2/3 cup no-salt-added tomato sauce
- 1 cup chopped plum tomatoes
- 1 1/2 cups frozen lima beans
- 3/4 teaspoon Italian seasoning, divided
- 2 1/4 cups reduced-sodium vegetable broth
- 1 cup chopped yellow bell pepper
- 3/4 teaspoon garlic powder, divided
- 3 pinches salt, divided

Instructions:

1. Get 3 1-pint jars. Divide the tomato sauce among these jars.
2. In each jar, top with 1/3 cup each of bell pepper, carrots, spinach, and tomatoes, as well as 1/2 cup lima beans. Cover the jars and place them in the fridge.
3. To prepare your soup, add 3/4 cup broth into a jar of the packed ingredients. Sprinkle 1/4 teaspoon of each of the following: garlic powder, Italian seasoning, and crushed red pepper. Also, add a pinch of salt. Microwave on high for 1 minute, then 2, and finally, 3 minutes.
4. Let the soup cool down before serving.
5. Enjoy!

Smoked Salmon–Stuffed Baked Potatoes

 Servings: 4   Total Time: 30 minutes

The combination of salmon and potatoes is good for regulating your blood pressure. This is due to the potassium in potatoes and the omega-3 fatty acids in salmon.

Nutritional Facts

256 calories   43 g carbohydrates
11 g proteins   5 g fats

Ingredients:

- 4 medium russet potatoes
- 4 ounces smoked salmon, cut into 1-inch pieces
- 1/2 cup red onion, thinly sliced
- 1/2 cup reduced-fat sour cream
- 4 teaspoons fresh chives, chopped
- 1 cup diced tomato

Instructions:

1. Use a fork to pierce the potatoes.
2. Microwave the potatoes on high for about 20 minutes. Turn them after every 5 minutes. Allow the potatoes to cool down on a cutting board.
3. Open the potatoes by cutting them in a lengthwise direction. Be sure not to cut them all the way through.
4. Top the potatoes with the salmon, sour cream, chives, onions, and tomatoes.
5. Serve and enjoy!

Chicken Chili Verde

 Servings: 6   Total Time: 30 minutes

The ingredients in this recipe help you take charge of your blood pressure. For instance, the protein and fiber in beans assist in controlling blood pressure.

Nutritional Facts

408 calories   41 g carbohydrates
32 g proteins   14 g fats

Ingredients:

- 2 15-ounce cans no-salt-added pinto beans, rinsed, divided
- 1 1/2 cups coarsely chopped fresh cilantro
- 4 cups unsalted chicken stock
- 2 cups chopped yellow onion
- 1 tablespoon canola oil
- 5 cloves garlic, chopped
- 1 1/2 pounds boneless, skinless chicken thighs, trimmed and cut into bite-size pieces
- 1 1/2 cups prepared salsa verde
- 2 cups chopped poblano peppers
- 2 cups chopped spinach
- 1/2 teaspoon salt
- 6 tablespoons sour cream
- 2 cups frozen corn kernels

Instructions:

1. Put a cup of beans in a bowl. Mash them.
2. Put a large pot on high heat and add oil. Add the chicken and cook for about 5 minutes. Be sure to occasionally turn the chicken as you cook.
3. Add the poblanos, garlic, and onion. Cook for about 5 more minutes.
4. Add salsa, salt, and stock, along with the mashed and whole beans. Bring to a boil before reducing the heat. Simmer and let the chicken cook for about 3 minutes.
5. Add spinach, cilantro, and corn. Cook for 1 more minute.
6. Top with the sour cream and serve.
7. Enjoy!

Green Goddess Salad With Chickpeas

 Servings: 2

 Total Time: 15 minutes

The fiber, minerals, and compounds in greens are beneficial to your heart health. The fiber in these plant-based ingredients helps to reduce the buildup of cholesterol in blood vessels.

Nutritional Facts

304 calories
22 g proteins

40 g carbohydrates
8 g fats

Ingredients:

For the dressing:
- 1 avocado, peeled and pitted
- 2 tablespoons rice vinegar
- 1 1/2 cups buttermilk
- 1/2 teaspoon salt
- 1/4 cup chopped fresh herbs

For the salad:
- 1/4 cup diced low-fat Swiss cheese
- 1 15-ounce can chickpeas, rinsed
- 3 cups chopped romaine lettuce
- 1 cup sliced cucumber

Instructions:

1. For the dressing, put the herbs, salt, avocado, buttermilk, and vinegar in a blender. Process until smooth.
2. For the salad, combine the cucumber, lettuce, and 1/4 cup of the dressing in a bowl.
3. Top with cheese, chickpeas, and tomatoes.
4. Serve and enjoy!

BBQ Baked Potatoes With Pork and Broccoli

🍽 Servings: 4   ⏱ Total Time: 30 minutes

The potassium and anthocyanins in potatoes, as well as flavonoids in broccoli, are supportive of healthy blood pressure levels.

Nutritional Facts

398 calories   53 g carbohydrates
21 g proteins   11 g fats

Ingredients:

- 4 medium russet potatoes (about 8 ounces each)
- 1 cup chopped steamed broccoli
- 1/2 cup barbeque sauce
- 4 teaspoons shredded sharp cheddar cheese
- 8 ounces shredded cooked pork, warmed

Instructions:

1. Use a fork to poke the potatoes. Microwave the potatoes on medium for 10 minutes. Flip them and microwave for 10 more minutes. Allow the potatoes to cool on a cutting board.
2. Cut the potatoes in a lengthwise direction, but don't cut all the way through.
3. Top the potatoes with pork, cheese, barbecue sauce, cheese, and broccoli.
4. Serve and enjoy!

Lemon Shrimp and Orzo Salad

 Servings: 4   Total Time: 20 minutes

This recipe is great for regulating blood cholesterol levels. The fiber in orzo and omega-3 fatty acids in the salmon ultimately reduce the levels of bad cholesterol in your blood. This saves you from conditions such as hypertension and heart disease.

Nutritional Facts

467 calories   50 g carbohydrates
33 g proteins   16 g fats

Ingredients:

- 2 teaspoons Dijon mustard
- 1 pound peeled and deveined raw shrimp (21–25 per pound), cut into bite-size pieces
- 8 ounces whole-wheat orzo
- Zest and juice of 1 lemon
- 4 cups sugar snap peas, cut into bite-size pieces
- 1/2 teaspoon ground pepper
- 1 tablespoon minced shallot
- 1/4 cup extra-virgin olive oil
- 1/2 teaspoon salt
- 1/4 cup finely chopped dill, plus more for garnish
- 1/2 teaspoon ground pepper

Instructions:

1. Add water to a large saucepan and bring to a boil. Cook the orzo for 7 minutes. Add the peas and shrimp and continue cooking for 3 more minutes. Drain.
2. Add the shallot, lemon juice and zest, pepper, dill, oil, salt, and mustard into a bowl. Whisk.
3. Add the peas, orzo, and shrimp into the bowl. Toss to mix.
4. Garnish with dill and serve.
5. Enjoy!

Creamy Pesto Chicken Salad with Greens

 Servings: 4   Total Time: 30 minutes

Nourish your body with the proteins, fiber, vitamins, and minerals from this recipe. The ingredients in this meal help to keep your blood pressure in check.

Nutritional Facts

324 calories   9 g carbohydrates
27 g proteins   20 g fats

Ingredients:

- 1 pound boneless, skinless chicken breast, trimmed
- 1/4 teaspoon salt
- 2 tablespoons extra-virgin olive oil
- 3 tablespoons finely chopped red onion
- 1/4 cup pesto
- 2 tablespoons red-wine vinegar
- 1/4 cup low-fat mayonnaise
- 1 5-ounce package mixed salad greens (about 8 cups)
- 1/4 teaspoon ground pepper
- 1 pint grape or cherry tomatoes, halved

Instructions:

1. Put the chicken in a saucepan. Add just enough water to cover the chicken by an inch.
2. Bring the ingredients to a boil before reducing the heat. Cover the pot and let the ingredients simmer for about 12 minutes.
3. Put the chicken on a cutting board and let it cool down. Shred the chicken into smaller pieces.
4. Add mayonnaise, onion, and pesto into a bowl. Mix and then add the chicken. Toss to coat.
5. Add salt, oil, pepper, and vinegar in a bowl. Whisk. Add the tomatoes and greens. Toss to coat.
6. Share the green salad among 4 plates. Top with the chicken.
7. Enjoy!

Black Bean and Slaw Bagel

 Servings: 2   Total Time: 10 minutes

Take advantage of the saponins in black beans and effectively lower the cholesterol levels in your body. This will help to keep your blood pressure under control.

Nutritional Facts

374 calories	61 g carbohydrates
15 g proteins	9 g fats

Ingredients:

- ⚙ 1 jalapeño-cheddar bagel, halved and toasted
- ⚙ 2 tablespoons lime juice
- ⚙ 2 cups shredded green cabbage
- ⚙ 1/2 avocado, mashed
- ⚙ 2 tablespoons chopped fresh cilantro
- ⚙ 1 cup rinsed no-salt-added canned black beans, heated
- ⚙ 1/8 teaspoon salt

Instructions:

1. Add the lime juice, cabbage, salt, and ciwo bagels.
2. Serve and enjoy!

SNACK RECIPES

Find the snack recipes in this section.

Cheddar-Apple Cracker Bites

 Servings: 4   Total Time: 5 minutes

The heart-healthy benefits of apples are not only attributed to the compounds they have but also what they lack. Looking at what they have, apples are fiber-rich, and this is good for your heart. On the other hand, apples do not have cholesterol, sodium, and saturated fats, all of which can negatively affect the health of your heart. Try this recipe and snack on this healthy ingredient!

Nutritional Facts

94 calories   16 g carbohydrates
3 g proteins   2 g fats

Ingredients:

- 1 tablespoon honey
- 2 slices reduced-fat cheddar cheese, cut into quarters
- 24 thin, vertical Fuji apple slices
- 2 teaspoons stone-ground mustard
- 8 flatbread crackers

Instructions:

1. Put a cheese quarter on each cracker before topping with three apple slices.
2. Mix mustard and honey in a bowl.
3. Drizzle this mixture over the apples.
4. Enjoy!

Pumpkin Pie Smoothie

 Servings: 1   Total Time: 5 minutes

Pumpkin is rich in various compounds that can promote better health for your heart. These include copper, folate, manganese, and fiber, as well as vitamins A, B1, B6, and C. Pumpkin also contains large amounts of potassium. The results from one study with 2,722 participants revealed that consuming larger amounts of potassium has similar effects to reducing the intake of sodium as far as blood pressure is concerned (Levings and Gunn, 2014).

Nutritional Facts

247 calories   42 g carbohydrates
10 g proteins   6 g fats

Ingredients:

- 1/3 cup canned pumpkin puree
- 2 teaspoons pure maple syrup
- 1/3 cup plain whole-milk Greek yogurt
- 1 medium frozen banana
- 1/8 teaspoon pumpkin pie spice
- 1/2 cup unsweetened almond milk

Instructions:

1. Add all the ingredients to a blender.
2. Process until the product is smooth.
3. Enjoy!

Savory Date and Pistachio Bites

 Servings: 32   Total Time: 10 minutes

Dates have soluble fiber, which makes them great for lowering the levels of LDL cholesterol, which is often associated with a higher risk of heart disease. The fiber in dates binds to the unwanted cholesterol, thereby making it unavailable for clogging your blood vessels. Imagine how this saves you from heart-related conditions such as high blood pressure!

Nutritional Facts

68 calories   13 g carbohydrates
1 g proteins   2 g fats

Ingredients:

- 2 cups whole dates, pitted
- 1/4 teaspoon ground pepper
- 1 cup golden raisins
- 1 cup raw pistachios, unsalted and shelled
- 1 teaspoon ground fennel seeds

Instructions:

1. Add fennel, dates, pepper, raisins, and pistachios in a food processor. Process until the ingredients appear finely chopped.
2. Take 1 tablespoon from the mixture and shape it into a ball. Repeat until all the mixture is finished.
3. Enjoy!

Bread With Peanut Butter

 Servings: 1   Total Time: 5 minutes

Some of the parameters that are important in maintaining a healthy heart are blood sugar, cholesterol, and blood pressure. Any food that helps to maintain healthy levels of these factors is good for your heart. Fair enough, peanut butter is one such food by virtue of the oleic acid that it contains.

Nutritional Facts

166 calories	16 g carbohydrates
7 g proteins	9 g fats

Ingredients:

- ⚙ 1 tablespoon peanut butter
- ⚙ 1 slice whole-wheat bread

Instructions:

1. Evenly spread the peanut butter on one side of the bread slice.
2. Enjoy!

Garlic Hummus

 Servings: 8   Total Time: 10 minutes

Chickpeas do not contain cholesterol, but they contain fiber. Both of these characteristics make chickpeas a good inclusion in your heart-healthy diet and the garlic hummus a great way of including these. Garlic may help to prevent your blood vessels from hardening as a result of atherosclerosis. By maintaining the flexibility of these vessels, garlic contributes to regulating blood pressure.

Nutritional Facts

155 calories   10 g carbohydrates
4 g proteins   12 g fats

Ingredients:

- 1 clove garlic
- 1 15-ounce can no-salt-added chickpeas
- 1/2 teaspoon chili powder
- 1/4 cup lemon juice
- 1 teaspoon ground cumin
- 1/4 cup extra-virgin olive oil
- 1/4 cup tahini
- 1/2 teaspoon salt

Instructions:

1. Partially drain the chickpeas, keeping half of the liquid.
2. Add the chickpeas, along with their liquid, into a food processor. Also, add chili powder, tahini, lemon juice, cumin, salt, garlic, and oil to the food processor.
3. Puree for about 3 minutes. The ingredients will appear well mixed and smooth.
4. Enjoy!

Smoked Salmon Toast

 Servings: 1 Total Time: 5 minutes

Give your body a treat by providing it with the healthy omega-3 fatty acids from the salmon. This fish will help to create a healthier balance of cholesterol in your body. Ideally, bad cholesterol levels will decrease while the good cholesterol levels rise. Your heart certainly needs that!

Nutritional Facts

82 calories   7 g carbohydrates
5 g proteins   4 g fats

Ingredients:

- ⚙ 1/2 ounce smoked salmon
- ⚙ 1 tablespoon Neufchâtel
- ⚙ 1 diagonal whole-wheat slice baguette
- ⚙ 1/4 teaspoon chopped fresh dill

Instructions:

1. Toast the bread slice.
2. Carefully top the bread slice with smoked salmon, dill, and Neufchâtel.
3. Enjoy!

Creamy Strawberry Smoothie

 Servings: 2   Total Time: 5 minutes

Strawberries are an indispensable ingredient when it comes to a heart-healthy diet. They help your body cells become more sensitive to insulin, which helps regulate the levels of glucose in your blood. Strawberries also reduce the concentrations of triglycerides in your blood. In large amounts, triglycerides can cause problems to your cardiovascular system. The berries also help to reduce the total amounts of bad cholesterol in your body.

Nutritional Facts

100 calories   16 g carbohydrates
6 g proteins   2 g fats

Ingredients:

- ☼ 1/4 teaspoon vanilla extract
- ☼ 3/4 cup low-fat milk
- ☼ 1 1/2 cups frozen strawberries
- ☼ 2 teaspoons honey
- ☼ 1/4 cup low-fat plain Greek

Instructions:

1. Add the honey, strawberries, yogurt, milk, and vanilla into a blender.
2. Process until the ingredients are smooth.
3. Enjoy!

Walnuts and Banana

 Servings: 1   Total Time: 5 minutes

Here is another excellent source of omega-3 fatty acids—walnuts. They contain a type of omega-3 fatty acid called alpha-linolenic acid, which is good for the health of your heart. Alpha-linolenic acid enhances a healthy cholesterol balance, alleviates inflammation, and significantly lowers high blood pressure. Not only that, alpha-linolenic acid is handy in cutting down the risk of heart disease (Watts, 2023). The heart-related benefits of the fiber-rich banana are a plus!

Nutritional Facts

236 calories   30 g carbohydrates
4 g proteins   13 g fats

Ingredients:

- 1 medium banana
- 10 walnut halves

Instructions:

1. Put your walnuts in a small bowl.
2. Eat them together with the banana.
3. Enjoy!

Cinnamon-Sugar Microwave Popcorn

 Servings: 1

 Total Time: 5 minutes

Cinnamon mainly promotes heart health in two ways. First, it does so directly by reducing the concentrations of unhealthy cholesterol in your body. Second, cinnamon does so indirectly by lowering your blood sugar levels. Normal blood sugar levels reduce the accumulation of bad cholesterol.

Nutritional Facts

130 calories
3 g proteins

21 g carbohydrates
5 g fats

Ingredients:

- A pinch of salt
- 1 teaspoon canola oil
- 1 1/2 tablespoons popcorn kernels
- 1/4 teaspoon ground cinnamon
- 1/2 teaspoon confectioners' sugar

Instructions:

1. Pack the popcorn kernels into a brown paper bag. Fold the top of the bag over about 3 times.
2. Put the paper bag into a microwave and process for about 1 1/2 minutes. You can stop microwaving once the popping stops.
3. Add cinnamon, oil, sugar, and salt into the paper bag. Hold the top of the bag and shake to coat the popcorn.
4. Enjoy!

Hard-Boiled Egg With Sauce

 Servings: 1   Total Time: 5 minutes

Boiling is one of the healthy cooking methods for eggs, especially when you are working on improving the health of your gut. An egg a day is good for your heart!

Nutritional Facts

78 calories	1 g carbohydrates
6 g proteins	5 g fats

Ingredients:

- ☼ 1 teaspoon sauce of choice
- ☼ 1 hard-boiled egg

Instructions:

1. Cut the egg into two halves.
2. Top it with the sauce of your choice.
3. Enjoy!

Cherry Tomato and Egg Cracker

 Servings: 1   Total Time: 10 minutes

If you're looking for a recipe that will assist in protecting the cells that line your blood vessels, this recipe is one of the alternatives you have at your disposal. Cherry tomatoes safeguard these endothelial cells, which are crucial in the structure of your blood vessels.

Nutritional Facts

78 calories   9 g carbohydrates
4 g proteins   3 g fats

Ingredients:

- 1 large crispbread
- 1/4 teaspoon black pepper, for garnish
- 2 cherry tomatoes, quartered
- 1/2 hard-boiled egg, diced

Instructions:

1. Add the eggs and tomatoes to the crispbread.
2. Garnish using black pepper.
3. Enjoy!

Homemade Trail Mix

 Servings: 5   ⏱ Total Time: 5 minutes

Think of this recipe as the "heart-healthy mix." All the ingredients included in this recipe have positive contributions to the well-being of your heart. For example, almonds, dates, and peanuts are associated with reduced cholesterol levels. Apricots offer antioxidants that protect the heart. And compounds in cranberries alleviate the risk of blood clot formation.

Nutritional Facts

132 calories   15 g carbohydrates
4 g proteins   7 g fats

Ingredients:

- 1/4 cup dried cranberries
- 2 ounces dried apricots
- 1/4 cup unsalted dry-roasted peanuts
- 1/4 cup whole shelled (unpeeled) almonds
- 1/4 cup chopped pitted dates

Instructions:

1. Mix the ingredients in a bowl.
2. Enjoy!

Carrot Cake Energy Bites

 Servings: 22   Total Time: 15 minutes

You can think of this recipe as your ultimate "heart-healthy" treat. The ingredients in this recipe collaborate toward a healthy heart system. Think of the pepper, cinnamon, ginger, oats, turmeric, chia seeds, and dates. Enjoy the combo!

Nutritional Facts

48 calories	8 g carbohydrates
1 g proteins	2 g fats

Ingredients:

- 1/4 teaspoon ground turmeric
- 1/2 cup old-fashioned rolled oats
- 1/4 cup chia seeds
- A pinch of ground pepper
- 3/4 teaspoon ground cinnamon
- 2 medium carrots, finely chopped
- 1/4 cup chopped pecans
- 1 teaspoon vanilla extract
- 1/2 teaspoon ground ginger
- 1/4 teaspoon salt
- 1 cup pitted dates

Instructions:

1. Add chia seeds, cinnamon, oats, dates, and pecans to a food processor. Pulse until the ingredients appear chopped and well combined.
2. Add turmeric, carrots, pepper, ginger, salt, and vanilla to the food processor. Process until the ingredients begin to form a paste.
3. Measure a tablespoon of the mixture and roll it into a ball. Do the same for the rest of the mixture.
4. Serve and enjoy!

Avocado Hummus

 Servings: 10   Total Time: 10 minutes

Research has shown that avocados are associated with a reduced risk of heart disease (Mahmassani et al., 2018). This is mainly attributed to the omega-3 fatty acids that the fruit contains. Enjoy these heart-healthy fats in this recipe!

Nutritional Facts

156 calories   10 g carbohydrates
3 g proteins   12 g fats

Ingredients:

- 1 clove garlic
- 1/4 cup extra-virgin olive oil
- 1 15-ounce can no-salt-added chickpeas
- 1/2 teaspoon salt
- 1/4 cup tahini
- 1 ripe avocado, halved and pitted
- 1 teaspoon ground cumin
- 1/4 cup lemon juice
- 1 cup fresh cilantro leaves

Instructions:

1. Drain the liquid from the chickpeas, but keep about 2 tablespoons of it.
2. Transfer the chickpeas together with the reserved liquid into a food processor. Add lemon juice, cilantro, cumin, avocado, salt, and tahini into the food processor with chickpeas.
3. Pulse until the ingredients appear smooth.
4. Serve along with veggie chips.
5. Enjoy!

Cottage Cheese Snack Jar

 Servings: 1   Total Time: 10 minutes

Cottage cheese is among the healthiest types of cheese as far as heart health is concerned. However, it's important to limit its intake, considering that it has relatively high sodium levels. This is especially true if you have been diagnosed with hypertension or congestive heart failure. The chickpeas in this recipe will help you control cholesterol levels in your body.

Nutritional Facts

219 calories   23 g carbohydrates
20 g proteins   5 g fats

Ingredients:

- 1/2 cup chopped cucumber
- 1/2 cup low-fat, no-salt-added cottage cheese
- 1/4 cup crunchy chickpeas

Instructions:

1. Get a 16-ounce glass container and put the cottage cheese in it.
2. Top the cheese with cucumber.
3. Add chickpeas.
4. Enjoy!

Blueberry-Lemon Energy Balls

 Servings: 6   Total Time: 10 minutes

Berries are potent antioxidant reservoirs. They are effective in scavenging oxidative radicals that could cause harm to your body, even to the cardiovascular system. Lemons add to this vitamin combo by providing vitamin C. According to research, food that is rich in vitamin C significantly cuts down the risk of stroke and heart disease (Chanet et al., 2012; Yokoyama et al., 2000).

Nutritional Facts

190 calories   27 g carbohydrates
4 g proteins   9 g fats

Ingredients:

- 1/2 cup pitted dates
- 3/4 cup walnuts
- 1 tablespoon lemon juice
- 1 teaspoon grated lemon zest
- 1/4 cup dried blueberries
- 2 tablespoons pure maple syrup
- 3/4 cup old-fashioned rolled oats

Instructions:

1. Add blueberries, walnuts, and dates to a food processor. Pulse for about 10 seconds until the ingredients are well-mixed and chopped.
2. Add lemon juice, oats, and maple syrup to the food processor. Pulse for about 30 more seconds. A thick paste should have formed by then.
3. Put the paste in a bowl before adding the lemon zest. Mix well.
4. Use the paste to roll 18 balls.
5. Enjoy!

Raspberry Yogurt Cereal Bowl

 Servings: 1   Total Time: 5 minutes

Raspberries contain manganese, potassium, and omega-3 fatty acids, all of which contribute to good heart health. Potassium regulates your blood pressure. Manganese controls your blood sugar, which is important for heart health. Omega-3 fatty acids enhance a healthier cholesterol balance that will keep your heart and blood vessels safe.

Nutritional Facts

290 calories   48 g carbohydrates
18 g proteins   5 g fats

Ingredients:

- 1/4 teaspoon ground cinnamon
- 1 cup nonfat plain yogurt
- 1/4 cup fresh raspberries
- 1 teaspoon pumpkin seeds
- 2 teaspoons mini chocolate chips
- 1/2 cup mini shredded-wheat cereal

Instructions:

1. Put yogurt in a serving bowl.
2. Top with pumpkin seeds, raspberries, shredded wheat, cinnamon, and chocolate chips.
3. Enjoy!

Tuna Salad Crackers

 Servings: 1   Total Time: 5 minutes

One of the diet-based strategies for preventing heart disease is by eating food rich in omega-3 fatty acids. Tuna fish is an excellent source of omega-3 fatty acids. These fats are heart-healthy, and they reduce the availability of bad cholesterol. You certainly need this for a healthy heart!

Nutritional Facts

297 calories   26 g carbohydrates
27 g proteins   9 g fats

Ingredients:

- 6 wheat crackers
- 1/2 cup cucumber slices
- 1 tablespoon reduced-fat olive oil mayonnaise
- 1 single-serve sun-dried-tomato hummus dip
- 1 2.6-ounce pouch low-sodium light tuna
- 1/2 cup red pepper strips

Instructions:

1. Mix mayonnaise and tuna into a bowl.
2. Spread the mayonnaise-tuna mixture on crackers.
3. Serve along with hummus, peppers, and cucumbers.
4. Enjoy!

Rice Cakes With Peanut Butter

 Servings: 1

 Total Time: 5 minutes

In this recipe, we recommend that you use brown rice instead of white. Research has shown that consuming white rice is associated with a rise in the risk of diabetes. On the contrary, brown rice has been reported to reduce the probability of having to deal with heart disease. The oleic acid in peanut butter adds to the heart health benefits that brown rice has.

Nutritional Facts

227 calories   19 g carbohydrates
7 g proteins   13 g fats

Ingredients:

- ☼ 2 multigrain rice cakes
- ☼ 1 1/2 tablespoons peanut butter

Instructions:

1. Evenly spread the peanut butter between the rice cakes.
2. Enjoy!

Mint, Lemon, and White Bean Dip

 Servings: 5   Total Time: 5 minutes

Mint exhibits anti-inflammatory and antioxidant properties. These attributes reduce the risk of heart disease. Mint, lemon, and white beans contain fiber, which helps to lower your blood sugar. The combination of these ingredients in one meal is good for your heart.

Nutritional Facts

144 calories   24 g carbohydrates
6 g proteins   3 g fats

Ingredients:

- 1 clove garlic
- 2 tablespoons fresh mint, chopped
- 1/4 teaspoon salt
- 1 tablespoon fresh lemon juice
- 1 15-ounce can no-salt cannellini beans, rinsed
- 1 tablespoon extra-virgin olive oil
- 1 teaspoon lemon zest
- 50 baby carrots
- 1/4 teaspoon black pepper, freshly ground

Instructions:

1. Add the garlic to a food processor and pulse until it's minced.
2. Add the lemon juice, pepper, beans, salt, mint, olive oil, and zest into the processor. Pulse again until the mixture becomes smooth. Cover and set aside.
3. Serve along with carrots.
4. Enjoy!

Peanut Butter–Banana Cinnamon Toast

 Servings: 1   Total Time: 5 minutes

You can imagine how much of a heart-healthy toast this is! Think of the oleic acid from the peanut butter, the fiber from the banana, and the cholesterol-reducing effects of cinnamon. Certainly, this is a must-try recipe, for your heart's sake!

Nutritional Facts

266 calories   38 g carbohydrates
8 g proteins   9 g fats

Ingredients:

- ☼ 1 small banana, sliced
- ☼ 1 slice whole-wheat bread, toasted
- ☼ Cinnamon, to taste
- ☼ 1 tablespoon peanut butter

Instructions:

1. Evenly spread the peanut butter over the toast.
2. Top with banana slices.
3. Sprinkle cinnamon over the banana slices.
4. Enjoy!

Chocolate-Banana Protein Smoothie

 Servings: 1   Total Time: 5 minutes

This smoothie is more than just a simple heart-healthy recipe; it's also a protein booster. Lentils have a wealth of proteins that your body can take advantage of for its repair and maintenance needs. In fact, proteins are also a good source of energy for heart-related processes. Not only that, but it has also been reported that increased consumption of proteins correlates with a lower risk of heart disease (Heart Foundation, 2016).

Nutritional Facts

310 calories   64 g carbohydrates
15 g proteins   2 g fats

Ingredients:

- ✿ 1 banana, frozen
- ✿ 2 teaspoons unsweetened cocoa powder
- ✿ 1/2 cup cooked red lentils
- ✿ 1 teaspoon pure maple syrup
- ✿ 1/2 cup nonfat milk

Instructions:

1. Add the syrup, banana, cocoa, milk, and lentils to a blender. Process until a smooth product results.
2. Serve and enjoy!

Almond-Stuffed Dates

 Servings: 1   Total Time: 5 minutes

Almonds can reduce the total cholesterol levels in your body. Stuffing them into dates is one of the creative ways to include these nuts in your meal plan. Dates also contain soluble fiber, so they also positively contribute to a healthy heart.

Nutritional Facts

149 calories	37 g carbohydrates
1 g proteins	1 g fats

Ingredients:

- ☼ 2 pitted Medjool dates
- ☼ 1/4 teaspoon orange zest
- ☼ 2 salted whole almonds

Instructions:

1. Stuff each almond into a separate date.
2. Roll the stuffed dates in orange zest.
3. Enjoy!

Cinnamon-Sugar-Roasted Chickpeas

 Servings: 4   Total Time: 55 minutes

This recipe will help you address blood pressure issues, if any. Chickpeas increase the concentration of bioavailable potassium in your body, and this is important for regulating the pressure at which your blood moves in the circulatory system. Prepare this recipe and keep cholesterol levels under control.

Nutritional Facts

125 calories   16 g carbohydrates
5 g proteins   5 g fats

Ingredients:

- 1 tablespoon sugar
- 1 15-ounce can chickpeas, rinsed
- 1 tablespoon avocado oil
- 1/8 teaspoon ground pepper
- 1 teaspoon ground cinnamon

Instructions:

1. Preheat your oven to 450 °F. Place your rack in the upper third level of the oven.
2. Pat the chickpeas with a paper towel and put them on the baking sheet. Spread them and bake for approximately 10 minutes.
3. Add pepper, sugar, and cinnamon into a bowl. Mix.
4. Transfer the roasted chickpeas into another bowl. Add oil and the cinnamon mixture into the same bowl. Toss the ingredients together.
5. Spread the coated chickpeas on the baking sheet again. Bake for about 20 more minutes. The chickpeas should appear crunchy and brownish by then.
6. Let the chickpeas cool down before serving.
7. Enjoy!

Almond Chia Blueberry Pudding

 Servings: 1   Total Time: 8 hours 10 minutes

In addition to the almonds and blueberries, this recipe introduces an ingredient that is crucial in heart health—chia seeds. These seeds have an antioxidant called quercetin, which may help in managing heart disease. The high amounts of fiber in chia seeds come in handy in regulating your blood pressure.

Nutritional Facts

229 calories   30 g carbohydrates
6 g proteins   11 g fats

Ingredients:

- 2 teaspoons pure maple syrup
- 1/2 cup fresh blueberries, divided
- 2 tablespoons chia seeds
- 1 tablespoon toasted slivered almonds, divided
- 1/8 teaspoon almond extract
- 1/2 cup unsweetened almond milk or other nondairy milk beverage

Instructions:

1. Add the maple syrup, almond milk, almond extract, and chia into a bowl. Mix well. Cover the bowl and refrigerate for about 8 hours. It's fine to leave the bowl in the fridge for up to 3 days.
2. Take the bowl out of the fridge and stir the pudding.
3. Transfer half of the pudding into a serving bowl. Top with half of the almonds and blueberries.
4. Add the remaining pudding to the bowl and top with the rest of the almonds and blueberries.
5. Enjoy!

Yogurt and Fruit Smoothie

 Servings: 1   Total Time: 10 minutes

When cholesterol builds up in the walls of your blood vessels, the condition is known as atherosclerosis. Under such circumstances, the space for the movement of blood becomes limited, which causes blood pressure to increase. Most fruits can reduce the levels of cholesterol that could accumulate inside your blood vessels, thereby alleviating the risk of atherosclerosis.

Nutritional Facts

279 calories   56 g carbohydrates
12 g proteins   2 g fats

Ingredients:

- 1/2 cup 100% pure fruit juice
- 3/4 cup nonfat plain yogurt
- 1 1/2 cups frozen fruit (blueberries, raspberries, pineapple or peaches)

Instructions:

1. Mix the juice and yogurt in a blender. Pulse until the mixture is smooth.
2. Without stopping the motor, add the fruit pieces through the opening on the lid. Continue processing until everything is smooth.
3. Enjoy!

Apple With Cinnamon Almond Butter

 Servings: 1   Total Time: 5 minutes

If you're looking for a quick snack that will energize you once more, this will help you achieve that, and it also helps you take care of your heart system. The unsaturated fats in almond butter have protective effects on your heart. Almond butter also keeps you feeling full for longer. This helps to control your calorie intake and blood sugar levels.

Nutritional Facts

193 calories   28 g carbohydrates
4 g proteins   9 g fats

Ingredients:

- 1 tablespoon smooth almond butter
- 1 medium apple
- A pinch of ground cinnamon

Instructions:

1. Carefully cut the apple into 8 slices that are relatively equal.
2. Spread some almond butter on each of the apple slices.
3. Sprinkle cinnamon over the apples.
4. Enjoy!

Hard-Boiled Egg and Almonds

 Servings: 1   Total Time: 5 minutes

The egg and almond combo is great for your heart system. Eating an egg a day can protect you from possible stroke and other heart-related conditions. Almonds reduce bad cholesterol and blood sugar levels. They also contain magnesium, which tends to improve hypertension (Schutten et al., 2018).

Nutritional Facts

181 calories   4 g carbohydrates
10 g proteins   14 g fats

Ingredients:

- 2 tablespoons unsalted dry-roasted almonds
- 1 hard-boiled egg
- A pinch of ground pepper
- A pinch of salt

Instructions:

1. Cut the boiled egg into two halves the long way.
2. Season the egg halves with pepper and salt.
3. Serve with almonds.
4. Enjoy!

This marks the end of the highlights of the recipes for your 28-day meal plan. In the next chapter, you will learn how to maintain the vibe and results that you have started to enjoy as a result of the "blood pressure" meal plan.

CHAPTER 6

Beyond the 28 Days

Finishing the 28-day meal plan doesn't mark the end of your efforts to maintain normal blood pressure levels. The journey continues, even beyond these 28 days. In fact, think of the 28-day meal plan as the first round of your training session for living a lifestyle that supports a healthy cardiovascular system. There is no harm in going for more such rounds. Play around with the meal plans and alter them to suit your needs and lifestyle. For instance, if you do strenuous work during the afternoon, you might need lunches that give you more energy. If so, alter the meal plans accordingly. The aim of this chapter is to ensure that we give you nuggets on how to continue maintaining a healthy heart system in the long term—maybe even for a lifetime.

Making Learned Habits Sustainable

Congratulations on making it through the 28-day meal plan! Now, the million-dollar question is, "How do I maintain the healthy habits that I learned and the results I achieved over the past four weeks?" The purpose of this section is to answer this question.

Try Mindful Shopping

Completing the 28-day meal plan is not a pass for binging and eating unhealthy foods now that you're done. Therefore, you still have to stick to healthy foods, and it all starts from your shopping sprees. Be sure to make healthy choices of foods by considering the following nuggets:

- **Shop around the walls.** Have you ever noticed that products such as lean meat, fruits, vegetables, and whole grains are usually arranged close to the walls in grocery stores? If yes, then shop around the walls and fill your baskets.
- **Avoid bulk packages.** While these might appear to be cheaper, they encourage overeating, making them more costly as far as your health is concerned. Instead, shop for smaller packages that will keep your food portions small.
- **Keep off the inside aisles.** You will find processed foods and other products that are relatively unhealthy in these aisles. If you want to keep these foods off your main diet, then stay off those aisles!
- **Avoid premade delicacies.** These could be sides or salads. These foods are usually rich in unhealthy fats and sodium, both of which are not good for your blood pressure and overall heart system.

Don't Go All Out When Eating Out

It's still possible to maintain a healthy eating lifestyle, even when you're eating out. Here are some tips to keep in mind:

- **Trick your stomach.** Start with salad, raw vegetables, or broth-based soup. This will help you gain an edge over your hunger and control the amount of food you consume.
- **Slow down.** This trick still applies even in the restaurant. Take your time to eat and properly chew every bite of your food.
- **Go for lean meat.** Even when you're served chicken, be sure to remove the skin and any fat. Never leave room for unhealthy fats!
- **Avoid the buffet.** This is a better way of avoiding scooping unhealthy delicacies into your plate. If you must go for a buffet, be sure to go for lean meat and green salads.

Keep It Heart-Healthy at Home

Remain conscious of the healthy lifestyle that you adopted during your 28-day meal plan. Here are some nuggets to keep in mind:

- **Do not eat when you don't experience the physical cues of hunger.** This means that you should avoid emotional and mental eating.
- **Keep your plates, bowls, and glasses small.** This assists you in reducing the likelihood of overeating.
- **Avoid piling food on your plate.** You could try to practice gratitude, avoid overwhelming scenarios, relax, and stay away from possible triggers. Just put enough to fill the plate and keep it that way.

Long-Term Lifestyle Changes for Addressing Hypertension

Coupling dietary changes with other nonmedication strategies will sustainably give you an edge on high blood pressure. In this section, we will discuss some of the strategies that you can employ to keep hypertension under control:

- **Engage in regular exercise.** Be it aerobic exercises, strength training, stretches, or yoga, just get your body moving. Even walking, jogging, dancing, cycling, or swimming will go a long way. Please note that strength training is particularly known for improving high blood pressure issues.
- **Do away with sodium and salt.** As you buy your ingredients and prepare your foods, avoid sodium and salt. Usually, 1,500 milligrams of sodium per day is good enough (Mayo Clinic, 2022). Anything above that may have disastrous effects on your blood pressure. Check food labels for sodium content. Also, it's always better not to add table salt.
- **Reduce alcohol intake and stop smoking.** Smoking and alcohol consumption raise your blood pressure beyond the normal range. If you can minimize these two, you will protect your cardiovascular system.
- **Effectively manage stress.** Since stress also elevates blood pressure, finding ways to manage it is a plus. Begin by identifying the root causes of your stress and then strategize on addressing them. You could try to practice gratitude, avoid overwhelming scenarios, relax, and stay away from possible triggers.
- **Improve the quality and quantity of your sleep.** Sleeplessness can contribute to hypertension. Ideally, adults are required to get seven to nine hours of sound sleep. Creating a sleep schedule that you will honor may be of help. Make your bedroom comfortable, quiet, dim, well-aerated, and peaceful to enhance a good night's sleep. We also recommend that you limit your day naps to no more than 30 minutes. Instead, try to sleep more during the night.

More Resources

Well done for getting to the end of this book! Feel free to look up more information about blood pressure using various resources. The following websites can provide you with authentic information that is well-researched:

- Center for Disease Control and Prevention
- Temple Health
- American Medical Association
- National Hypertension Control Initiative
- Medical News Today
- WebMD

You can also consider reading journal articles that focus on blood pressure. The easiest way to find journal articles is by visiting Google Scholar. Use relevant search words that align with what you are looking for to narrow down your search.

Conclusion

Nutrients from food play a vital role in regulating blood pressure. For example, potassium and magnesium help blood vessels relax, a state that reduces the pressure at which blood flows in your blood vessels. Omega-3 fatty acids are a healthy type of fat that influence the cholesterol balance in your body. They increase the levels of good cholesterol (HDL) while reducing those of bad cholesterol (LDL). Bad cholesterol can clog blood vessels, leading to a condition referred to as *atherosclerosis*. Blocked blood vessels interfere with the normal flow of the blood, thereby causing hypertension. The fatty plaques may also narrow the lumen of the blood vessels, thereby reducing the volume that flows through them at any given time. This means that your heart will have to pump harder to maintain adequate supplies of oxygen and nutrients to the rest of your body.

Fiber makes you feel full for longer periods, which reduces your calorie intake, thereby regulating blood sugar levels. Remember, any excess blood sugar is ultimately converted to fat for storage, some of which is deposited in and around your blood vessels. Simply put, fiber helps to prevent the accumulation of fat in your body, and this contributes to reducing high blood pressure.

The involvement of nutrients in addressing blood pressure issues implies that diet is an important factor as far as blood pressure is concerned. This is why you should be careful in selecting ingredients for your meals. Generally, fruits, vegetables, lean meat, nuts, and whole grains offer the nutrients that support your cardiovascular health. However, selecting healthy foods is not enough. Incorporating mindful eating and intuitive eating presents a holistic approach to addressing high blood pressure. Mindful eating brings your senses along as you focus on your meals. It allows you to enjoy the taste, smell, appearance, and texture of your food so that you get the best out of it. Mindful eating improves your self-awareness, which helps you to connect positively with your food. As you continue with this practice, you will adopt better, healthier eating habits that will benefit your cardiovascular system.

Intuitive eating helps you connect to your hunger and satiety cues. It makes it easier for you to determine the physical signals that tell you that you are truly hungry. These include lightheadedness, losing concentration, a rumbling stomach, headaches, and/or stomachaches. Intuitive eating allows you to differentiate between actual hunger and other forms that are associated with mental and emotional aspects. While actual hunger can be set off by eating, this is not the same with the other types, which may remain, no matter how much food you eat.

This book also introduced the concept of intermittent fasting as a tool for addressing high blood pressure. Be sure to adopt an intermittent fasting approach that doesn't cause your blood pressure to drop too low, such as the ones that require you to refrain from eating for up to 24 hours. For women, experts suggest that you choose intermittent fasting methods with fasting windows that do not exceed 14 hours. The day-fasting strategies are commendable because then you don't have to miss meals.

To wrap it all up, this book unleashed a 28-day meal plan with 112 different recipes. Use the step-by-step descriptions of the recipes to make enjoyable meals that will not only grace your taste buds but help you maintain normal blood pressure levels. After your 28-day meal plan, be sure to maintain the positive results that you have already achieved by consistently following the mindful and intuitive eating principles.

It's time to take the bull by the horns and take charge of your blood pressure and overall cardiovascular health. Start now and live to enjoy the results for a lifetime!

Refrences

Alderson, E. (2024, July 21). *Old-fashioned oatmeal*. EatingWell. https://www.eatingwell.com/recipe/269639/old-fashioned-oatmeal/

Alkhalifah, M. K., Alabduljabbar, K. A. & Alkhenizan, A. H. (2021). Effect of natural honey on lowering lipid profile. *Saudi Medical Journal, 42*(5), 473–480. https://doi.org/10.15537/smj.2021.42.5.20200664

Amdur, E. (2022, October 4). *"The illiterate of the 21st century…"* Forbes. https://www.forbes.com/sites/eliamdur/2022/10/04/the-illiterate-of-the-21st-century/

Ball, J. (2023, September 19). *Charred shrimp, pesto and quinoa bowls*. EatingWell. https://www.eatingwell.com/recipe/274095/charred-shrimp-pesto-quinoa-bowls/

Bashinsky, R. (2018a). *Chicken, brussels sprouts and mushroom salad*. EatingWell. https://www.eatingwell.com/recipe/269828/chicken-brussels-sprouts-mushroom-salad/

Bashinsky, R. (2018b). *Chicken chili verde*. EatingWell. https://www.eatingwell.com/recipe/269830/chicken-chili-verde/

Bashinsky, R. (2018c). *Seitan BBQ sandwiches*. EatingWell. https://www.eatingwell.com/recipe/269837/seitan-bbq-sandwiches/

Bashinsky, R. (2023, September 19). *Spinach and egg scramble with raspberries*. EatingWell. https://www.eatingwell.com/recipe/269838/spinach-egg-scramble-with-raspberries/

Benjamim, C. J. R., Porto, A. A., Valenti, V. E., Sobrinho, A. C. da S., Garner, D. M., Gualano, B. & Bueno Júnior, C. R. (2022). Nitrate derived from beetroot juice lowers blood pressure in patients with arterial hypertension: A systematic review and meta-analysis. *Frontiers in Nutrition, 9*. https://doi.org/10.3389/fnut.2022.823039

Bondonno, C. P., Dalgaard, F., Blekkenhorst, L. C., Murray, K., Lewis, J. R., Croft, K. D., Kyrø, C., Torp-Pedersen, C., Gislason, G., Tjønneland, A., Overvad, K., Bondonno, N. P. & Hodgson, J. M. (2021). Vegetable nitrate intake, blood pressure and incident cardiovascular disease: Danish Diet, Cancer, and Health Study. *European Journal of Epidemiology*. https://doi.org/10.1007/s10654-021-00747-3

Burns, C. & Kidron, A. (2020). *Biochemistry, tyramine*. PubMed; StatPearls Publishing. https://www.ncbi.nlm.nih.gov/books/NBK563197/

Casner, C. (2016). *Smoked turkey, kale, and rice bake*. EatingWell. https://www.eatingwell.com/recipe/250591/smoked-turkey-kale-rice-bake/

Casner, C. (2022). *Lemon-garlic vegetable soup*. EatingWell. https://www.eatingwell.com/recipe/7997988/lemon-garlic-vegetable-soup/

Casner, C. (2023a, September 18). *Creamy strawberry smoothie*. EatingWell. https://www.eatingwell.com/recipe/7961991/creamy-strawberry-smoothie/

Casner, C. (2023b, September 19). *Tomato, cucumber and white-bean salad with basil vinaigrette*. EatingWell. https://www.eatingwell.com/recipe/265886/tomato-cucumber-white-bean-salad-with-basil-vinaigrette/

Casner, C. (2024a, January 31). *Teriyaki chicken skillet casserole with broccoli is on the table in 30 minutes*. EatingWell. https://www.eatingwell.com/teriyaki-chicken-skillet-casserole-with-broccoli-8404232

Casner, C. (2024b, April 19). *Cinnamon-sugar roasted chickpeas*. EatingWell. https://www.eatingwell.com/recipe/267759/cinnamon-sugar-roasted-chickpeas/

Casner, C. (2024c, April 19). *Herbal chamomile health tonic*. EatingWell. https://www.eatingwell.com/recipe/261083/herbal-chamomile-health-tonic/

Casner, C. (2024d, April 19). *Pineapple-grapefruit detox smoothie*. EatingWell. https://www.eatingwell.com/recipe/269497/pineapple-grapefruit-detox-smoothie/

Casner, C. (2024e, April 22). *Baked fish tacos with avocado*. EatingWell. https://www.eatingwell.com/recipe/263566/baked-fish-tacos-with-avocado/

Casner, C. (2024f, April 22). *Blueberry almond chia pudding*. EatingWell. https://www.eatingwell.com/recipe/258456/blueberry-almond-chia-pudding/

Casner, C. (2024g, April 24). *Two-ingredient banana pancakes*. EatingWell. https://www.eatingwell.com/recipe/268783/two-ingredient-banana-pancakes/

Casner, C. (2024h, July 5). *Chopped power salad with chicken*. EatingWell. https://www.eatingwell.com/recipe/7917784/chopped-power-salad-with-chicken/

Chanet, A., Milenkovic, D., Manach, C., Mazur, A. & Morand, C. (2012). Citrus Flavanones: What Is Their Role in Cardiovascular Protection? *Journal of Agricultural and Food Chemistry, 60*(36), 8809–8822. https://doi.org/10.1021/jf300669s

Chatto, J. (2016). *Fassoulatha (white bean soup)*. EatingWell. https://www.eatingwell.com/recipe/247583/fassoulatha-white-bean-soup/

Cleveland Clinic. (n.d.). *Fast eater? 4 tips to help you slow down*. Cleveland Clinic. https://health.clevelandclinic.org/why-do-i-eat-so-fast

Corliss, J. (2021, October 1). *Eating more whole grains linked to lower heart-related risks*. Harvard Health. https://www.health.harvard.edu/heart-health/eating-more-whole-grains-linked-to-lower-heart-related-risks

Davis, E. (2024, April 18). *Pistachio and peach toast*. EatingWell. https://www.eatingwell.com/recipe/267207/pistachio-peach-toast/

Diabetic Living Magazine. (2023a, September 19). *Bread with Peanut Butter*. EatingWell. https://www.eatingwell.com/recipe/263538/bread-with-peanut-butter/

Diabetic Living Magazine. (2023b, September 19). *Southwestern waffle*. EatingWell. https://www.eatingwell.com/recipe/269368/southwestern-waffle/

Dolge, A. (2024a, April 18). *Egg tartine*. EatingWell. https://www.eatingwell.com/recipe/7913503/egg-tartine/

Dolge, A. (2024b, April 18). *Miso-maple salmon*. EatingWell. https://www.eatingwell.com/recipe/276374/miso-maple-salmon/

Dolge, A. (2024c, April 18). *Pan-seared steak with crispy herbs and escarole*. EatingWell. https://www.eatingwell.com/recipe/275771/pan-seared-steak-with-crispy-herbs-escarole/

Dolge, A. (2024d, May 10). *Slow-cooker chicken and white bean stew*. EatingWell. https://www.eatingwell.com/recipe/269820/slow-cooker-chicken-white-bean-stew/

Dolge, A. (2024e, July 21). *Lemon shrimp and orzo salad*. EatingWell. https://www.eatingwell.com/recipe/279674/lemon-shrimp-orzo-salad/

Eating Well Kitchen. (2024a, March 28). *Lemon, mint and white bean dip*. EatingWell. https://www.eatingwell.com/lemon-mint-white-bean-dip-7972390

Eating Well Kitchen. (2024b, April 19). *Marinara meat sauce topped baked potato*. EatingWell. https://www.eatingwell.com/recipe/259434/marinara-meat-sauce-topped-baked-potato/

Eating Well Test Kitchen. (2018). *Cabbage, tofu and edamame salad*. EatingWell. https://www.eatingwell.com/recipe/266430/cabbage-tofu-edamame-salad/

Eating Well Test Kitchen. (2019). *Pork and green chile stew*. EatingWell. https://www.eatingwell.com/recipe/269916/pork-green-chile-stew/

Eating Well Test Kitchen. (2023a, September 19). *Cherry tomato & egg cracker*. EatingWell. https://www.eatingwell.com/recipe/264175/cherry-tomato-egg-cracker/

Eating Well Test Kitchen. (2023b, September 19). *Orange-ginger tea*. EatingWell. https://www.eatingwell.com/recipe/265917/orange-ginger-tea/

Eating Well Test Kitchen. (2023c, September 19). *Red beans and rice with chicken*. EatingWell. https://www.eatingwell.com/recipe/262999/red-beans-and-rice-with-chicken/

Eating Well Test Kitchen. (2023d, September 19). *Tuna salad crackers*. EatingWell. https://www.eatingwell.com/recipe/266426/tuna-salad-crackers/

Eating Well Test Kitchen. (2024a, March 28). *Cheddar-apple cracker bites*. EatingWell. https://www.eatingwell.com/cheddar-apple-cracker-bites-7972354

Eating Well Test Kitchen. (2024b, April 18). *Pecan butter and pear toast*. EatingWell. https://www.eatingwell.com/recipe/7916856/pecan-butter-pear-toast/

Eating Well Test Kitchen. (2024c, April 19). *Italian zucchini-topped baked potato*. EatingWell. https://www.eatingwell.com/recipe/259491/italian-zucchini-topped-baked-potato/

Eating Well Test Kitchen. (2024d, April 22). *Baby kale breakfast salad with smoked trout and avocado*. EatingWell. https://www.eatingwell.com/recipe/251411/baby-kale-breakfast-salad-with-smoked-trout-avocado/

Eating Well Test Kitchen. (2024e, April 22). *Green goddess salad with chickpeas*. EatingWell. https://www.eatingwell.com/recipe/258450/green-goddess-salad-with-chickpeas/

Eating Well Test Kitchen. (2024f, April 22). *Southwestern salad with black beans*. EatingWell. https://www.eatingwell.com/recipe/250230/southwestern-salad-with-black-beans/

Eating Well Test Kitchen. (2024g, July 10). *Creamy blueberry-pecan oatmeal*. EatingWell. https://www.eatingwell.com/recipe/251104/creamy-blueberry-pecan-oatmeal/

Eating Well Test Kitchen. (2024h, July 23). *Fruit and yogurt smoothie*. EatingWell. https://www.eatingwell.com/recipe/249318/fruit-yogurt-smoothie/

Eetplan. (2021, September 29). *Top tips for maintaining a healthy goal weight*. The 28 Day Diet. https://the28daydiet.co.za/top-tips-for-maintaining-a-healthy-goal-weight/

El Khoury, D., Cuda, C., Luhovyy, B. L. & Anderson, G. H. (2012). Beta Glucan: Health Benefits in obesity and metabolic syndrome. *Journal of Nutrition and Metabolism, 2012*, 1–28. https://doi.org/10.1155/2012/851362

Ellison, D. H. & Terker, A. S. (2015). Why your mother was right: How potassium intake reduces blood pressure. *Transactions of the American Clinical and Climatological Association, 126*, 46–55. https://www.ncbi.nlm.nih.gov/pmc/articles/PMC4530669/

Fakhri, S., Patra, J. K., Das, S. K., Das, G., Majnooni, M. B. & Farzaei, M. H. (2021). Ginger and heart health: from mechanisms to therapeutics. *Current Molecular Pharmacology, 14*(6), 943–959. https://doi.org/10.2174/1874467213666201209105005

Fantin, Macchi, Giani & Bissoli. (2019). The importance of nutrition in hypertension. *Nutrients, 11*(10), 2542. https://doi.org/10.3390/nu11102542

Fletcher, J. (2022, February 4). *What is the link between hypertension (high blood pressure), heart disease, and stroke?* Medicalnewstoday.com; Medical News Today. https://www.medicalnewstoday.com/articles/how-are-hypertension-heart-disease-and-stroke-related

Fountaine, S. (2024a, April 22). *Rainbow grain bowl with cashew tahini sauce.* EatingWell. https://www.eatingwell.com/recipe/260740/rainbow-buddha-bowl-with-cashew-tahini-sauce/

Fountaine, S. (2024b, April 22). *Roasted vegetable and black bean tacos.* EatingWell. https://www.eatingwell.com/recipe/257722/roasted-vegetable-black-bean-tacos/

Frothingham, S. (2019, August 29). *Blood pressure after eating, plus other factors that affect readings.* Healthline. https://www.healthline.com/health/blood-pressure-after-eating

Haas, S. (2024a, April 11). *Apple with cinnamon almond butter.* EatingWell. https://www.eatingwell.com/recipe/251354/apple-with-cinnamon-almond-butter/

Haas, S. (2024b, April 18). *Almond-stuffed dates.* EatingWell. https://www.eatingwell.com/recipe/254638/almond-stuffed-dates/

Haas, S. (2024c, April 18). *Peanut butter and chia berry jam english muffin.* EatingWell. https://www.eatingwell.com/recipe/255160/peanut-butter-chia-berry-jam-english-muffin/

Haas, S. (2024d, April 18). *Raspberry yogurt cereal bowl.* EatingWell. https://www.eatingwell.com/recipe/257116/raspberry-yogurt-cereal-bowl/

Haas, S. (2024e, April 18). *Tex-mex pasta salad.* EatingWell. https://www.eatingwell.com/recipe/273194/tex-mex-pasta-salad/

Haas, S. (2024f, April 18). *Tex-mex pasta salad.* EatingWell. https://www.eatingwell.com/recipe/273194/tex-mex-pasta-salad/

Haas, S. (2024g, June 4). *This cottage cheese snack jar is packed with 20 grams of protein.* EatingWell. https://www.eatingwell.com/recipe/8078448/cottage-cheese-snack-jar/

Hartley, M., Fyfe, C. L., Wareham, N. J., Khaw, K.-T., Johnstone, A. M. & Myint, P. K. (2022). Association between Legume Consumption and Risk of Hypertension in the European Prospective Investigation into Cancer and Nutrition (EPIC)-Norfolk Cohort. *Nutrients, 14*(16), 3363. https://doi.org/10.3390/nu14163363

Harvard Health Publishing. (2019a, May 3). *Key minerals to help control blood pressure.* Harvard Health; Harvard Health. https://www.health.harvard.edu/heart-health/key-minerals-to-help-control-blood-pressure

Harvard Health Publishing. (2019b, June 24). *Are eggs risky for heart health?* Harvard Health; Harvard Health. https://www.health.harvard.edu/heart-health/are-eggs-risky-for-heart-health

Heart Foundation. (2016). *Protein and heart health.* Heartfoundation.org.au. https://www.heartfoundation.org.au/healthy-living/healthy-eating/protein-and-heart-health

Hendley, J. (2024, April 22). *Homemade trail mix.* EatingWell. https://www.eatingwell.com/recipe/248712/homemade-trail-mix/

Hodges, C. (2024a, April 19). *3-ingredient broccoli mac and cheese with rotisserie chicken.* EatingWell. https://www.eatingwell.com/recipe/7915446/3-ingredient-broccoli-mac-cheese-with-rotisserie-chicken/

Hodges, C. (2024b, April 22). *Hearty tomato soup with beans and greens.* EatingWell. https://www.eatingwell.com/recipe/269888/hearty-tomato-soup-with-beans-greens/

Hodges, C., M.S. & RDN. (2024, April 19). *Loaded black bean nacho soup.* EatingWell. https://www.eatingwell.com/recipe/269841/loaded-black-bean-nacho-soup/

Holland, K. (2017, October 17). *Why does my blood pressure fluctuate?* Healthline. https://www.healthline.com/health/fluctuating-blood-pressure#treatment

Ito, K., Miyata, K., Mohri, M., Origuchi, H. & Yamamoto, H. (2017). The effects of the habitual consumption of miso soup on the blood pressure and heart rate of Japanese adults: A cross-sectional study of a health examination. *Internal Medicine, 56*(1), 23–29. https://doi.org/10.2169/internalmedicine.56.7538

Joshipura, K. J., Hu, F. B., Manson, J. E., Stampfer, M. J., Rimm, E. B., Speizer, F. E., Colditz, G., Ascherio, A., Rosner, B., Spiegelman, D. & Willett, W. C. (2001). The effect of fruit and vegetable intake on risk for coronary heart disease. *Annals of Internal Medicine, 134*(12), 1106. https://doi.org/10.7326/0003-4819-134-12-200106190-00010

Khalesi, S., Irwin, C. & Schubert, M. (2015). Flaxseed consumption may reduce blood pressure: A systematic review and meta-analysis of controlled trials. *The Journal of Nutrition, 145*(4), 758–765. https://doi.org/10.3945/jn.114.205302

Killeen, B. (2019, December). *Mushroom and tofu stir-fry.* EatingWell. https://www.eatingwell.com/recipe/277158/mushroom-tofu-stir-fry/

Killeen, B. (2024a, April 18). *Classic sesame noodles with chicken.* EatingWell. https://www.eatingwell.com/recipe/254642/classic-sesame-noodles-with-chicken/

Killeen, B. (2024b, April 18). *Creamy pesto chicken salad with greens.* EatingWell. https://www.eatingwell.com/recipe/251161/creamy-pesto-chicken-salad-with-greens/

Killeen, B. (2024c, April 22). *Chocolate-banana protein smoothie.* EatingWell. https://www.eatingwell.com/recipe/267647/chocolate-banana-protein-smoothie/

Killeen, B. (2024d, April 22). *Smoked salmon cheese toast.* EatingWell. https://www.eatingwell.com/recipe/251301/smoked-salmon-cheese-toast/

Killeen, B. (2024e, April 25). *Muesli with raspberries.* EatingWell. https://www.eatingwell.com/recipe/265712/muesli-with-raspberries/

Killeen, B. L. (2024, April 19). *Chickpea pasta with mushrooms and kale.* EatingWell. https://www.eatingwell.com/recipe/7939117/chickpea-pasta-with-mushrooms-kale/

Kim, S. H., Thomas, M. J., Wu, D., Carman, C. V., Ordovás, J. M. & Meydani, M. (2019). Edible mushrooms reduce atherosclerosis in Ldlr−/− mice fed a high-fat diet. *The Journal of Nutrition, 149*(8), 1377–1384. https://doi.org/10.1093/jn/nxz075

Kirkland, A. (2024, July 22). *Walnut-rosemary crusted salmon*. EatingWell. https://www.eatingwell.com/recipe/267223/walnut-rosemary-crusted-salmon/

Lastowka, L. (2019). *Salmon couscous salad*. EatingWell. https://www.eatingwell.com/recipe/270571/salmon-couscous-salad/

Leopold, J. A. (2015). Antioxidants and coronary artery disease. *Coronary Artery Disease, 26*(2), 176–183. https://doi.org/10.1097/mca.0000000000000187

Levings, J. L. & Gunn, J. P. (2014). The imbalance of sodium and potassium intake: implications for dietetic practice. *Journal of the Academy of Nutrition and Dietetics, 114*(6), 838–841. https://doi.org/10.1016/j.jand.2014.02.015

Levy, J. (2023). *Shrimp paella*. EatingWell. https://www.eatingwell.com/recipe/8031576/shrimp-paella/

Levy, J. (2024, June 20). *Anti-inflammatory chicken and beet salad*. EatingWell. https://www.eatingwell.com/recipe/8063667/chicken-beet-salad/

Lipton, B. (2024, March 8). *Carrot cake energy bites*. EatingWell. https://www.eatingwell.com/recipe/273188/carrot-cake-energy-bites/

Llanaj, E., Dejanovic, G. M., Valido, E., Bano, A., Gamba, M., Kastrati, L., Minder, B., Stojic, S., Voortman, T., Marques-Vidal, P., Stoyanov, J., Metzger, B., Glisic, M., Kern, H. & Muka, T. (2022). Effect of oat supplementation interventions on cardiovascular disease risk markers: a systematic review and meta-analysis of randomized controlled trials. *European Journal of Nutrition, 61*(4), 1749–1778. https://doi.org/10.1007/s00394-021-02763-1

Lopez, W. (2023, September 23). *Blueberry-lemon energy balls*. EatingWell. https://www.eatingwell.com/recipe/7964794/blueberry-lemon-energy-balls/

Loucks, E. B., Kronish, I. M., Saadeh, F. B., Scarpaci, M. M., Proulx, J. A., Gutman, R., Britton, W. B. & Schuman-Olivier, Z. (2023). Adapted mindfulness training for interoception and adherence to the DASH diet: A phase 2 randomized clinical trial. *JAMA Network Open, 6*(11), e2339243. https://doi.org/10.1001/jamanetworkopen.2023.39243

Madsen, H., Sen, A., & Aune, D. (2023). Fruit and vegetable consumption and the risk of hypertension: a systematic review and meta-analysis of prospective studies. *European Journal of Nutrition*. https://doi.org/10.1007/s00394-023-03145-5

Mahmassani, H. A., Avendano, E. E., Raman, G., & Johnson, E. J. (2018). Avocado consumption and risk factors for heart disease: a systematic review and meta-analysis. *The American Journal of Clinical Nutrition, 107*(4), 523–536. https://doi.org/10.1093/ajcn/nqx078

Makhijani, P. (2024, April 18). *Saucy ginger-tomato chicken*. EatingWell. https://www.eatingwell.com/recipe/7938725/saucy-ginger-tomato-chicken/

Malcoun, C. (2018). *Crunchy chicken and mango salad*. EatingWell. https://www.eatingwell.com/recipe/265729/crunchy-chicken-mango-salad/

Malcoun, C. (2024a, April 18). *Greek salad with edamame*. EatingWell. https://www.eatingwell.com/recipe/257315/greek-salad-with-edamame/

Malcoun, C. (2024b, April 22). *Cream of turkey and wild rice soup*. EatingWell. https://www.eatingwell.com/recipe/252422/cream-of-turkey-wild-rice-soup/

Malcoun, C. (2024c, July 30). *Lemony linguine with spring vegetables*. EatingWell. https://www.eatingwell.com/recipe/262750/lemony-linguine-with-spring-vegetables/

Mayo Clinic. (2022, July 12). *10 drug-free ways to control high blood pressure*. Mayo Clinic. https://www.mayoclinic.org/diseases-conditions/high-blood-pressure/in-depth/high-blood-pressure/art-20046974

Meyer, H. (2023, September 19). *No-cook black bean salad*. EatingWell. https://www.eatingwell.com/recipe/265885/no-cook-black-bean-salad/

Meyer, H. (2024, April 19). *Berry-banana cauliflower smoothie*. EatingWell. https://www.eatingwell.com/recipe/265882/berry-banana-cauliflower-smoothie/

Morrow, S. (2024). *Southwest chopped salad with tomatillo dressing*. EatingWell. https://www.eatingwell.com/recipe/7938225/southwest-chopped-salad-with-tomatillo-dressing/

O'Brien, D. (n.d.). *Everything bagel avocado toast*. EatingWell. https://www.eatingwell.com/recipe/261631/everything-bagel-avocado-toast/

O'Brien, D. (2019). *BBQ baked potatoes with pork & broccoli*. EatingWell. https://www.eatingwell.com/recipe/275784/bbq-baked-potatoes-with-pork-broccoli/

O'Brien, D. (2022, April 18). *Spinach, peanut butter and banana smoothie*. EatingWell. https://www.eatingwell.com/recipe/280738/spinach-peanut-butter-banana-smoothie/

O'Brien, D. (2024a, March 28). *Garlic hummus*. EatingWell. https://www.eatingwell.com/recipe/256571/garlic-hummus/

O'Brien, D. (2024b, April 18). *Mango raspberry smoothie*. EatingWell. https://www.eatingwell.com/recipe/280734/mango-raspberry-smoothie/

O'Brien, D. (2024c, April 18). *Smoked salmon stuffed baked potatoes*. EatingWell. https://www.eatingwell.com/recipe/275786/smoked-salmon-stuffed-baked-potatoes/

O'Brien, D. (2024d, April 22). *Avocado hummus*. EatingWell. https://www.eatingwell.com/recipe/256572/avocado-hummus/

O'Brien, D. (2024e, April 22). *Cinnamon-sugar microwave popcorn*. EatingWell. https://www.eatingwell.com/recipe/269221/cinnamon-sugar-microwave-popcorn/

Ozemek, C., Laddu, D. R., Arena, R. & Lavie, C. J. (2018). The role of diet for prevention and management of hypertension. *Current Opinion in Cardiology, 33*(4), 388–393. https://doi.org/10.1097/hco.0000000000000532

Parmar, R. (2022, March 2). *12 incredible health benefits of bananas*. PharmEasy Blog. https://pharmeasy.in/blog/12-incredible-health-benefits-of-bananas/

Ried, K. (2019). Garlic lowers blood pressure in hypertensive subjects, improves arterial stiffness and gut microbiota: A review and meta-analysis. *Experimental and Therapeutic Medicine, 19*(2). https://doi.org/10.3892/etm.2019.8374

Sandoval-Ramírez, B. A., Catalán, Ú., Calderón-Pérez, L., Companys, J., Pla-Pagà, L., Ludwig, I. A., Romero, M. P. & Solà, R. (2020). The effects and associations of whole-apple intake on diverse cardiovascular risk factors. A narrative review. *Critical Reviews in Food Science and Nutrition*, 60(22), 3862–3875. https://doi.org/10.1080/10408398.2019.1709801

Schutten, J. C., Joosten, M. M., de Borst, M. H. & Bakker, S. J. L. (2018). Magnesium and blood pressure: A physiology-based approach. *Advances in Chronic Kidney Disease*, 25(3), 244–250. https://doi.org/10.1053/j.ackd.2017.12.003

Seaver, V. (2014, April 19). *Yogurt with blueberries and honey*. EatingWell. https://www.eatingwell.com/recipe/261617/yogurt-with-blueberries-honey/

Seaver, V. (2023, September 19). *Rice cakes with peanut butter*. EatingWell. https://www.eatingwell.com/recipe/261621/rice-cakes-with-peanut-butter/

Seaver, V. (2024a, April 19). *Banana and walnuts*. EatingWell. https://www.eatingwell.com/recipe/261622/banana-walnuts/

Seaver, V. (2024b, April 19). *Hard-boiled egg with hot sauce*. EatingWell. https://www.eatingwell.com/recipe/261613/hard-boiled-egg-with-hot-sauce/

Seaver, V. (2024c, June 5). *Peanut butter-banana cinnamon toast*. EatingWell. https://www.eatingwell.com/recipe/261628/peanut-butter-banana-cinnamon-toast/

Shariq, O. A. & McKenzie, T. J. (2020). Obesity-related hypertension: a review of pathophysiology, management, and the role of metabolic surgery. *Gland Surgery*, 9(1), 80–93. https://doi.org/10.21037/gs.2019.12.03

Slagle, A. (2024, April 22). *Savory Date & Pistachio Bites*. EatingWell. https://www.eatingwell.com/recipe/268714/savory-date-pistachio-bites/

Smith, J. (2024). *Anti-inflammatory eat-the-rainbow vegetable soup (meal-prep friendly)*. EatingWell. https://www.eatingwell.com/eat-the-rainbow-vegetable-soup-8391242

Tang, H., Cao, Y., Yang, X. & Zhang, Y. (2020). Egg consumption and stroke risk: A systematic review and dose-response meta-analysis of prospective studies. *Frontiers in Nutrition*, 7. https://doi.org/10.3389/fnut.2020.00153

Taste of Home. (2022a, March 11). *Berry granola pancakes*. Taste of Home. https://www.tasteofhome.com/recipes/berry-granola-pancakes/

Taste of Home. (2022b, March 15). *Whole wheat pancakes*. Taste of Home. https://www.tasteofhome.com/recipes/whole-wheat-pancakes/

Taste of Home. (2022c, August 9). *Portobello mushrooms florentine*. Taste of Home. https://www.tasteofhome.com/recipes/portobello-mushrooms-florentine/

Taste of Home. (2022d, August 9). *Southwest tortilla scramble*. Taste of Home. https://www.tasteofhome.com/recipes/southwest-tortilla-scramble/

Taste of Home. (2023a, March 8). *Carrot cake oatmeal*. Taste of Home. https://www.tasteofhome.com/recipes/carrot-cake-oatmeal/

Taste of Home. (2023b, July 12). *Spiced blueberry quinoa*. Taste of Home. https://www.tasteofhome.com/recipes/spiced-blueberry-quinoa/

Taste of Home. (2023c, September 12). *Breakfast sweet potatoes*. Taste of Home. https://www.tasteofhome.com/recipes/breakfast-sweet-potatoes/

Taste of Home. (2023d, September 23). *Lemon chia seed parfaits*. Taste of Home. https://www.tasteofhome.com/recipes/lemon-chia-seed-parfaits/

Turpin, A. S. (2024a, April 12). *Black bean and slaw bagel*. EatingWell. https://www.eatingwell.com/recipe/7920673/black-bean-slaw-bagel/

Turpin, A. S. (2024b, April 18). *Cannellini bean and herbed ricotta toast*. EatingWell. https://www.eatingwell.com/recipe/7920759/cannellini-bean-herbed-ricotta-toast/

University, U. S. (n.d.). *Learning to listen to hunger and fullness cues*. Extension.usu.edu. https://extension.usu.edu/nutrition/research/learning-listening-hunger-fullness-cues

Upham, B. (2024, July 31). *Combining mindfulness and the heart-healthy DASH diet can significantly improve blood pressure*. EverydayHealth.com. https://www.everydayhealth.com/heart-health/mindfulness-training-helps-people-eat-a-more-heart-healthy-diet/

Valente, L. (2024, April 19). *Pumpkin pie smoothie*. EatingWell. https://www.eatingwell.com/recipe/260736/pumpkin-pie-smoothie/

Vendrame, S. & Klimis-Zacas, D. (2019). Potential factors influencing the effects of anthocyanins on blood pressure regulation in humans: A review. *Nutrients, 11*(6). https://doi.org/10.3390/nu11061431

Vinmec International Hospital. (n.d.). *Does eating ginger increase blood pressure?* Vinmec International Hospital. https://www.vinmec.com/eng/article/does-eating-ginger-increase-blood-pressure-en

Visuanath, V. (2024). *This high-fiber salad is inspired by Indian street food and helps me manage my blood sugar*. EatingWell. https://www.eatingwell.com/bhel-puri-inspired-salad-8645205

Wallace, T. C. (2011). Anthocyanins in cardiovascular disease. *Advances in Nutrition, 2*(1), 1–7. https://doi.org/10.3945/an.110.000042

Wang, L., Tao, L., Hao, L., Stanley, T. H., Huang, K.-H., Lambert, J. D. & Kris-Etherton, P. M. (2019). A moderate-fat diet with one avocado per day increases plasma antioxidants and decreases the oxidation of small, dense ldl in adults with overweight and obesity: A randomized controlled trial. *The Journal of Nutrition, 150*(2). https://doi.org/10.1093/jn/nxz231

Warren, R. M. (2023, September 23). *Strawberry spinach salad with avocado and walnuts*. EatingWell. https://www.eatingwell.com/recipe/273198/strawberry-spinach-salad-with-avocado-walnuts/

Watts, E. (2023, March 26). *1 cup of walnuts a day may boost heart health via the gut*. Www.medicalnewstoday.com. https://www.medicalnewstoday.com/articles/walnuts-for-heart-health-effect-on-the-gut-may-be-key#What-do-the-experts-say?

Webster, K. (2016). *Bean salad with lemon-cumin dressing*. EatingWell. https://www.eatingwell.com/recipe/252725/bean-salad-with-lemon-cumin-dressing/

Webster, K. (2017, August). *Chickpea and quinoa grain bowl*. EatingWell. https://www.eatingwell.com/recipe/259822/chickpea-quinoa-buddha-bowl/

Webster, K. (2022, October 7). *Veggie and hummus sandwich*. EatingWell. https://www.eatingwell. com/recipe/259817/veggie-hummus-sandwich/

Webster, K. (2024a, April 22). *Mason jar power salad with chickpeas and tuna*. EatingWell. https:// www.eatingwell.com/recipe/263360/mason-jar-power-salad-with-chickpeas-tuna/

Webster, K. (2024b, April 22). *Mixed greens with lentils and sliced apple*. EatingWell. https://www. eatingwell.com/recipe/259816/mixed-greens-with-lentils-sliced-apple/

World Health Organisation (WHO). (2023, March 16). *Hypertension*. World Health Organization. https://www.who.int/news-room/fact-sheets/detail/hypertension

Wouk, J., Dekker, R. F. H., Queiroz, E. A. I. F. & Barbosa-Dekker, A. M. (2021). β-Glucans as a panacea for a healthy heart? Their roles in preventing and treating cardiovascular diseases. *International Journal of Biological Macromolecules, 177*, 176–203. https://doi.org/10.1016/j. ijbiomac.2021.02.087

Yokoyama, T., Date, C., Kokubo, Y., Yoshiike, N., Matsumura, Y. & Tanaka, H. (2000). Serum vitamin c concentration was inversely associated with subsequent 20-year incidence of stroke in a japanese rural community. *Stroke, 31*(10), 2287–2294. https://doi.org/10.1161/01. str.31.10.2287

Yoo, D. & Park, Y. (2020). Association between the intake of fermented soy products and hypertension risk in postmenopausal women and men aged 50 years or older: The Korea National Health and Nutrition Examination Survey 2013–2018. *Nutrients, 12*(12), 3621. https://doi.org/10.3390/nu12123621

Yuan, X., Wang, J., Yang, S., Gao, M., Cao, L., Li, X., Hong, D., Tian, S. & Sun, C. (2022). Effect of intermittent fasting diet on glucose and lipid metabolism and insulin resistance in patients with impaired glucose and lipid metabolism: A systematic review and meta-analysis. *International Journal of Endocrinology, 2022*, 1–9. https://doi.org/10.1155/2022/6999907

Zhu, B., Haruyama, Y., Muto, T. & Yamazaki, T. (2015). Association between eating speed and metabolic syndrome in a three-year population-based cohort study. *Journal of Epidemiology, 25*(4), 332–336. https://doi.org/10.2188/jea.je20140131

Zhu, Y., Bo, Y., Wang, X., Lu, W., Wang, X., Han, Z. & Qiu, C. (2016). The Effect of Anthocyanins on Blood Pressure. *Medicine, 95*(15), e3380. https://doi.org/10.1097/md.0000000000003380

Image Refrences

Abdullah, S. (2020). Maintaining good habits [Image]. *Pixabay*. https://pixabay.com/photos/keys-yes-no-keyboard-computer-5170080/

Congerdesign. (2019). Ginger [Image]. *Pixabay*. https://pixabay.com/photos/ginger-ginger-tea-hot-drink-drink-3966502/

Efrainstochter. (2015). Listen to your body cues [Image]. *Pixabay*. https://pixabay.com/photos/headphones-green-listen-to-music-641186/

Entstresser. (2017). Hard-boiled egg [Image]. *Pixabay*. https://pixabay.com/photos/egg-breakfast-boiled-egg-brown-bowl-2404597/

Gadini. (2015). Blood pressure [Image]. *Pixabay*. https://pixabay.com/photos/pressure-device-meter-blood-pressure-990462/

Ignartonosbg. (2022). Red beans [Image]. *Pixabay*. https://pixabay.com/photos/red-beans-vegetables-legumes-beans-7228265/

JohnyVid. (2024). Avocado [Image]. *Pixabay*. https://pixabay.com/photos/avocado-food-fruit-vegetables-8498520/

Karyna, P. (2022). Chickpeas [Image]. *Pixabay*. https://pixabay.com/photos/chickpeas-snack-organic-healthy-7003521/

Larisa K. (2015). Apples [Image]. *Pixabay*. https://pixabay.com/photos/apples-basket-fruits-apple-basket-805124/

LauraLisLT. (2017). Sweet potatoes [Image]. *Pixabay*. https://pixabay.com/photos/sweet-potato-food-vegetable-yam-2086784/

LC-Click. (2019). Blueberries [Image]. *Pixabay*. https://pixabay.com/photos/blueberries-fruits-food-fresh-4011294/

Lernestorod. (2017). Shrimp [Image]. *Pixabay*. https://pixabay.com/photos/shrimp-paella-prawns-crustaceo-2393818/

MaisonBoutarin. (2018). Garlic [Image]. *Pixabay*. https://pixabay.com/photos/garlic-cloves-vegetable-produce-3185163/

Muzamil496. (2023). Cardiovascular health [Image]. *Pixabay*. https://pixabay.com/photos/human-heart-heart-organ-anatomy-8274822/

Pentrenz. (2021). Raspberries [Image]. *Pixabay*. https://pixabay.com/photos/fruits-raspberries-berries-food-6357256/

PhotoMIX Company. (2016). Beet [Image]. *Pixabay*. https://pixabay.com/photos/red-beets-vegetables-leaves-1725799/

Shutterbug75. (2016). Broccoli [Image]. *Pixabay*. https://pixabay.com/photos/broccoli-food-green-healthy-leaf-1239149/

Silviarita. (2017). Healthy food [Image]. *Pixabay*. https://pixabay.com/photos/salad-fruit-berry-healthy-vitamins-2756467/

Tortic84. (2017). Tomato soup [Image]. *Pixabay*. https://pixabay.com/photos/tomato-soup-soup-gazpacho-2288056/

Tseiu. (2016). Walnuts [Image]. *Pixabay*. https://pixabay.com/photos/pecans-nut-walnut-1214706/

Made in United States
Troutdale, OR
04/30/2025

30984590R10089